Triumph over Shyness

Triumph over Shyness

Conquering Shyness and Social Anxiety

Murray B. Stein, MD

John R. Walker, PhD

Copublished with the Anxiety Disorders Association
of America

McGraw-Hill

New York   Chicago   San Francisco   Lisbon   London
Madrid   Mexico City   Milan   New Delhi
San Juan   Seoul   Singapore
Sydney   Toronto

McGraw-Hill

A Division of The McGraw·Hill Companies

Library of Congress Cataloging-in-Publication Data

Stein, Murray B.
    Triumph over shyness: conquering shyness and social anxiety / Murray B. Stein, John
R. Walker.
      p. cm.
    Includes bibliographical references and index.
    ISBN 0-07-137498-1
    1. Bashfulness. 2. Anxiety. 3. Social phobia. 4. Interpersonal relations. I. Walker, John
R., 1949- II. Title.

BF575.B3 S74 2001
155.2'32—dc21   2001037049

1 2 3 4 5 6 7 8 9 0   DOC/DOC   0 9 8 7 6 5 4 3 2 1

ISBN 0-07-137498-1

This book was set in Minion by North Market Street Graphics.

Printed and bound by R.R. Donnelley & Sons Company.

Throughout this book, trademarked names are used. Rather than put a trademark symbol
after every occurrence of a trademarked name, we use names in an editorial fashion only,
and to the benefit of the trademark owner, with no intention of infringement of the trademark. Where such designations appear in this book, they have been printed with initial caps.

This publication is designed to provide accurate and authoritative information in regard to
the subject matter covered. It is sold with the understanding that the publisher is not engaged
in rendering psychological, medical, or other professional service. If expert assistance or
counseling is required, the services of a competent professional person should be sought.
      —Adapted from a declaration of principles jointly adopted by a committee
           of the American Bar Association and a committee of publishers.

 This book is printed on recycled, acid-free paper containing a minimum of 50%
recycled de-inked fiber.

McGraw-Hill books are available at special quantity discounts to use as premiums and sales
promotions, or for use in corporate training programs. For more information, please write
to the Director of Special Sales, Professional Publishing, McGraw-Hill, Two Penn Plaza,
New York, NY 10121-2298. Or contact your local bookstore.

To Orah, Rebecca, Nathan, and Dorit.
For all you've taught me.
MBS

To Joannie, Ian, and Andrea.
For your love and support.
JRW

Contents

Part Three: Improving Your Relationships   151

Preface

The meek shall inherit the Earth.
Psalms 37:11

Speak softly and carry a big stick.
Theodore Roosevelt

There's nothing wrong with being shy. The world needs some quiet, thoughtful, introspective people. People who don't shoot (off their mouths) first and ask questions later (or never). People who are reluctant to intrude and careful not to offend.

So if you're shy and proud of it, read something else. Buy this book if you want to—the proceeds go to a worthy cause (our retirement funds)—and give it to someone who is bothered by social anxiety.

And there's the rub. Many people aren't happy about being shy. They find it prevents them from expressing themselves, from making friends, and from enjoying life to its fullest. For some people, shyness is a cocoon. It's safe and warm and quiet. But it can also be confining, dark, and lonely. If you choose to triumph over shyness, this book will help you break free.

Acknowledgments

Thanks:

To our editor, Robin Cantor-Cooke, for challenging us to do our best writing (and for showing us how when we weren't up to the task).

To our many patients and clients who have taught us so much about courage in overcoming anxiety.

To Jerilyn Ross and the Anxiety Disorders Association of America for asking us to write this book.

To all the people who provided feedback on chapters (knowingly or unknowingly), including (in alphabetical order) Tarek Afifi, Lois Callander, Denise Chavira, Jason Ediger, Trish Furer, Jennifer Garinger, Shadha Hami, Beverley Joyce, Michelle Kozey, Carrie Lionberg, Adrienne Means-Christensen, Tracy Morris, Jitender Sareen, Kathryn Sexton, Orah Stein, Laine Torgrud, and Michelle Warren.

To Mary Glenn, our editor at McGraw-Hill, for overseeing the final product.

To our students, colleagues, and friends who have shared their ideas with us and helped us shape ours.

Triumph over Shyness

Part One

Understanding Shyness and Social Anxiety

CHAPTER 1

The Most Common Fear

W e all know shy people. Some of us—many of us, in fact—consider ourselves shy. Over 20 years ago, Philip Zimbardo, a well-known psychologist at Stanford University, asked his students whether they were shy. He found that about one in three people described himself or herself as shy. This is probably as true now as it was then. In fact, there is some reason to believe that severe forms of shyness may even be on the upswing.

When people are asked about their greatest fears, speaking in public is very high on the list, with about one in five reporting an extreme fear of public speaking. Fear of public speaking is a form of what we call *social anxiety.*

So we know that shyness and social anxiety are extremely common. And we now know that shyness and social anxiety prevent some people from living life as fully as they would like to. This book is for those people. It is also for parents who have a child with these problems, and for people concerned about a friend or family member with these problems.

Before we delve deeper into social anxiety disorder, let's introduce some concepts and define some terms we'll be using throughout the book.

What Are Shyness and Social Anxiety?

Shyness refers to a tendency to withdraw from people, particularly unfamiliar people. It is a normal personality trait. This means that everyone has some degree of shyness—some people have a lot, some have a little, and most have an amount somewhere in between. Think of it as you would height. Height is a physical trait. Some people are tall, some are short, but most are somewhere in between. Height is one of those physical traits that are largely heritable—that is, due to the effect of genes. These genes come from your biological parents. You are born with a predetermined likelihood of being a particular height. Height is also influenced by factors such as diet and perhaps the amount of stress in the environment.

Shyness, like height, is influenced by genes. We'll discuss this more in the next chapter, but for the moment, the important thing to realize is that shyness is a trait. Other traits include personal characteristics like hair color, eye color, perfectionism, the tendency to look for excitement (sometimes called *novelty seeking*), and intelligence. With the exception of hair color and eye color, few of these traits are influenced *exclusively* by genes. The things we learn throughout life and the experiences we have—and the choices we make—can strongly influence the vast majority of human traits.

Most personality and physical traits are *normally distributed* (a statistical term) throughout the population. What does this mean? It means that if we were to take all the people in the world and measure how much of a particular trait they each have, we would usually find that the trait follows the so-called bell-shaped curve. This is as true of shyness as it is of anything else. If we took a sample of 1000 people and measured their shyness (perhaps with a questionnaire, or by videotaping them and analyzing their behavior), we'd likely find something that looks like the bell-shaped curve shown in Fig. 1.1.

What we see from this diagram is that some people are very shy (on the far right of the curve), and some people are not very shy at all (on the far left of the curve). Most people are somewhere in between. It is possible that possessing a great deal (or very little) of a trait can cause problems for a person. We know that some people who are very shy have difficulties related to their shyness. Some of these people find that their shyness prevents them from doing things they would like to be able to do, such as getting out and making new friends, assuming greater positions of responsibility at work, and the like.

We know considerably less about the people on the far left of the bell-shaped curve. Is there such a thing as not having enough shyness? This has

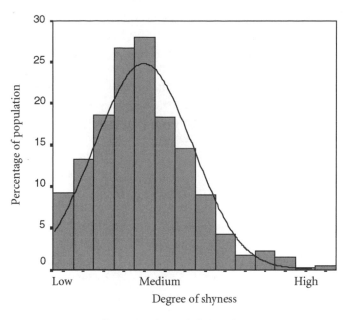

Figure 1.1 Shyness bell-shaped curve.

not been studied, to the best of our knowledge. But we might speculate, for example, that someone who isn't "shy enough" might be oblivious to the feelings of others and come across as insensitive or callous. At its extreme, might some people with very low shyness become criminals because of their fearlessness of others? Nobody knows.

Social anxiety is closely affiliated with though not identical to shyness. We should start by defining *anxiety*. Anxiety is an uncomfortable internal state (that is, something people feel inside) usually associated with uncertainty or the unknown. Anxiety is an emotion. Anxiety is a lot like *fear,* but fear is what you feel when you *know* what you're afraid of. When someone points a gun at your head, you don't feel anxiety. You feel fear! You know exactly what it is that is causing your heart to race, your knees to shake, and your life to flash before your eyes. When you exit the door of your house to take out the garbage at night, you may feel anxious, wondering if someone is lurking in the shadows waiting to attack you. This is anxiety, not fear, because you don't know whether something bad is going to happen; you think it is a possibility, but you can't be sure. So you feel anxious about it.

(If you live in a major metropolitan area with lots of crime, this may not be such a good example, but you get the point.) Anxiety is an emotion you feel when you believe there *might* be a threat; fear is an emotion you feel when you know there *is* a threat.

Social anxiety refers to the special kind of anxiety or discomfort you may experience when you are around other people. Usually, social anxiety is associated with concerns about being scrutinized. When you are around other people and you worry about what they think of you and you feel uncomfortable, you are experiencing social anxiety. As you might imagine, the notion of social anxiety overlaps tremendously with shyness, as well as with other concepts, such as *self-consciousness.*

There are some differences between the concepts of shyness and social anxiety, at least in the ways those of us who study behavior and mental health use these terms. Shyness is something that is often inferred by observing behavior. For example, psychologists may videotape people at a party, then review the tapes and use a stopwatch to see how long it takes each person to approach a stranger and join or initiate a conversation. They may infer that people who are more reticent to do this are shyer than those who jump right in. In fact, the researchers wouldn't know anything about what the partygoers were thinking or feeling—in order to know this, they'd need to ask them. But psychologists observe and measure people's behaviors to make inferences about their degree of shyness.

This may be valid or it may not. There could be all sorts of reasons why someone might take longer to join in a conversation at a party. These reasons could range from being shy, to being bored, to being preoccupied because of a recent argument with his or her spouse, to not being fluent in the language spoken at the party. Because of these uncertainties, some researchers would say that we shouldn't really call this inferred behavior *shyness*, but rather something like *slowness to join a conversation,* or *behavioral reticence,* or *social avoidance.* But shyness is what we often call it, nonetheless, particularly when we see these behaviors in children.

Social anxiety, on the other hand, isn't something that can be inferred. It's not enough to observe a person's behavior—say, the fact that someone doesn't speak up as much as his or her colleagues at a meeting—and come to the conclusion that this is because the person is socially anxious. In order to know whether people are socially anxious—or to measure precisely how anxious they are—you need to ask them. Anxiety—any kind of anxiety—is an internal state. It is something people feel. It's not something they wear on their sleeves, and it's not something we can measure with a machine. But if we could, we'd call the machine an anxietometer, start a company (anxietyprovoking.com), go public, and retire. But we digress. The point is that social anxiety is something that people feel; it's not something that can be observed by others. (Remember this. We'll come back to it later.)

Embarrassment and Shame: Kissing Cousins to Social Anxiety and Shyness?

At this point, it is important to introduce a couple of additional concepts that overlap to some extent those we have already covered. Some of you might wonder, for example, where *embarrassment* fits into this discussion, but you might be too embarrassed to ask. Don't be. It's a good question. Entire books have been written about embarrassment. One by Rowland Miller, a psychology professor at Sam Houston State University in Texas, is particularly enlightening. Miller defines embarrassment as a basic emotion, "that state of awkward abashment and chagrin that results from public events that disrupt our expectations and communicate unwanted impressions of ourselves to others. It is an uncomfortable emotion that will be avoided if possible." Embarrassment, according to this definition, is an emotion you might feel if your pants fell down while you were giving a sales presentation. Unlike social anxiety or shyness, which can occur in anticipation of a social event (for instance, worrying about going to a party because you may be faced with talking with unfamiliar people), embarrassment is more reactive, and has much more of the element of surprise associated with it (for example, finding out when you arrive at a party that Halloween was last week, and you're the only one wearing a costume).

You may be wondering, "Aren't people who are socially anxious worried about being embarrassed?" Yes, indeed. Fear of embarrassment—the fear of doing or saying something that will draw attention to oneself—is a core fear of people with social anxiety. Do people who are shy or socially anxious become more easily embarrassed than people who are not shy or socially anxious? The answer is not clear. But shy people certainly *worry* a lot more about the possibility that this might happen.

Shame is an emotion closely connected to embarrassment. Some theorists argue that embarrassment is merely a milder form of shame: If your pants droop a bit when you're giving your talk, you feel embarrassed, whereas if they fall precipitously to the floor and reveal your Donald Duck underwear, you feel ashamed. Others feel that shame is a deeper, darker emotion, wherein people feel that their experience has revealed to them something about their inner selves, something they're not proud of.

Let's illustrate this distinction:

A middle-aged man is leaving a coffeehouse with a tall, no-foam, extra-sugar, double-shot, overpriced vanilla latte when he trips over a skateboard. He doesn't fall, but spills the latte on his pants in an area usually reflective of poor bladder control. People outside the coffeehouse are looking at him, and he feels embarrassed. He strides up to a teenager having a tall, extra-foam, no-sugar, nonfat triple very overpriced cappuccino, and yells, "Why don't you take care of your damn toys? I could've been hurt!" He then storms away, gets into his car, and drives off. He feels ashamed of himself for his behavior toward the teenager, and berates himself for losing his temper.

Embarrassment, then, is what you feel when something (often unexpected) draws unwanted attention to you. *Shame* is what you feel when you are disappointed in yourself. Embarrassment, though intensely unpleasant, is fleeting. Shame is more enduring and, worse yet, it accumulates. People who are socially anxious worry a lot about being embarrassed. And they go out of their way to avoid having this happen. Some people with social anxiety, perhaps especially those with social anxiety so severe it interferes with their lives, may also carry around an inordinate burden of shame.

Terminology

Does all this concern with terminology seem like verbal hair-splitting? It does to us, at times. But there's a good reason for it. Investigators may study various aspects of the same phenomenon and label them differently. Investigators who study children and behavioral genetics tend to focus on *shyness,* while those who study abnormal adult behavior and mental disorders concentrate on *social anxiety.* And not all researchers agree on the definitions of the distinctions they make. Some experts, including Mark Leary, a psychology professor at Wake Forest University, believe that shyness is merely a combination of social anxiety and social reticence. Leary uses the terms *social anxiety* and *shyness* interchangeably, as we will at times in this book. We will be careful to distinguish, however, the difference between a normal personality trait like shyness, which can run the gamut from low to high, and an abnormal condition such as *social anxiety disorder* (also known as *social phobia*), which is marked by unusually high levels of social anxiety and associated difficulties.

Anxiety Is a Normal Response:
How Much Is Enough?

Anxiety is a normal response to situations that are stressful or involve uncertain threat. It serves as a signal that says, "Hey, you! Pay attention! Be careful! Something might go wrong." This is not a bad thing. If we had no anxiety at all, we'd all be so mellow that we'd probably never get off the couch. (Okay, maybe just to eat.) Without anxiety, we'd go boldly where no one should go. We'd be oblivious to potentially dangerous situations—we'd drive through red lights, we'd spend more money than we have, we'd go mountain climbing without the proper gear. (Having grown up in Manitoba, Canada's answer to Kansas, we really have no idea what a mountain looks like, much less an inclination to climb one without gear. Or with gear, for that matter.) Anxiety can be a motivator, if it's not so overwhelming that it paralyzes. If we had no anxiety, we'd never be motivated to try harder at play; we'd never complete our assignments at work. A little bit of anxiety, when it serves to spur us to do better, is a good thing. A lot of anxiety, however, is not. How much anxiety is enough?

That's a very difficult question to answer. Anxiety that is neither persistent nor overwhelming nor intrusive (it doesn't get in the way of the things you want to do) is enough. In the case of social anxiety, it's enough if it helps you be aware of and attentive to the opinions and feelings of others. It's enough if it contributes to your desire to achieve, to do well not only in your own opinion but also in the opinion of those around you. It's enough if it leads you to prepare appropriately for a professional conference by learning beforehand who the other participants will be, and memorizing the names of their spouses and children so that you can make them (and yourself) feel more comfortable.

But if social anxiety leads you to worry for weeks ahead of time about the conference, that's too much. If your child can't sleep for three nights prior to presenting a five-minute oral book report at school, that's too much. If you are not able to concentrate when you're in a group of two or three people, that's too much.

Jeffrey: "I don't think I could handle college."

Jeffrey is an 18-year-old high school senior from a middle-class home. His parents work full time, Dad as a school principal, and Mom as a receptionist in a dental office. He has a younger sister in eighth grade and a brother in fifth.

Jeffrey gets good grades, mostly As and Bs, and his strength is mathematics. He is six feet tall, and most people would describe him as good-looking, although he doesn't think of himself this way. He has a couple of good friends whom he has known since first or second grade, but few beyond that. He doesn't go to parties and has not dated, though he expresses an interest in girls and says he would like to date.

Jeffrey avoids taking courses that involve making presentations in front of the class. This started at age 13, when he developed severe acne. He became very self-conscious about his appearance and avoided being seen in public. He had no choice but to attend school, but he sat at the back of the room and didn't hang out with kids during lunch hour or after school. He was fortunate in that new acne medications became available right around that time; his skin condition was well controlled, and he was left with no discernible scarring.

But at age 18, Jeffrey is still acutely self-conscious. He admits he isn't concerned only about his appearance; he worries about drawing any kind of attention to himself for fear that he might do or say something to embarrass himself. This has led him to make any excuse he can think of to avoid speaking in class. He deliberately chooses courses that involve written rather than oral reports. When there is no choice, he calls in sick; in most cases, he is permitted to hand in a written report later. Whenever possible, he works behind the scenes on group presentations: he does the research, the writing, the drawing, and the typing, and lets others present the work.

Jeffrey must now think seriously about where he is going to go to college and, indeed, whether he is going at all. His parents are eager for him to go; his teachers feel he has the ability, and his grades certainly support this opinion. But Jeffrey isn't sure. He is aware that in order to succeed in college, he needs to be able to speak in front of others. Moreover, he will need to move out of his small, comfortable social circle and meet new people.

Jeffrey feels incapable of doing these things. He knows others can't understand the magnitude of the terror he feels when he has to answer a question in class. They can't imagine the white fear that leaves him sweating and shaking at the mere thought of approaching a girl he thinks is attractive, and maybe even attracted to him. No one, he believes, can fathom how he blames himself for his perceived weakness, and how ashamed he is.

There is no doubt that Jeffrey's shyness is extreme, and that it has become a major problem for him. Not only does he experience social anxiety in anticipation of many social situations, but he also often avoids these situations if he can. Moreover, he is extremely upset by his inability to do things he would like to do, and blames himself for these shortcomings. Jeffrey's social anxiety has become a major force that limits what he can do now, and what future choices he will make for himself regarding his education and career.

Jeffrey's shyness has reached a level that would cause a mental health professional to label it pathological, meaning that it is far beyond normal, and causing a lot of distress and negative consequences. When this happens, we say a person is suffering from *social phobia,* also known as *social anxiety disorder.*

A *phobia* is an unreasonable or irrational fear. Common phobias are snake phobias, height phobias, and flying phobias. And one of the most common of all is social phobia.

What Is Social Phobia (Also Known as Social Anxiety Disorder)?

According to the fourth edition of the American Psychiatric Association's *Diagnostic and Statistical Manual of Mental Disorders* (*DSM-IV*), the primary diagnostic system used by North American mental health professionals, social phobia consists of "a marked and persistent fear of one or more social or performance situations in which the person is exposed to unfamiliar people or to possible scrutiny by others. The individual fears that he or she will act in a way (or show anxiety symptoms) that will be humiliating or embarrassing. . . ."

When people with social phobia are faced with a situation where others might observe them, they experience extreme anxiety. This anxiety can take the form of a *panic attack,* an acute episode of anxiety marked by extreme discomfort, and physical symptoms such as a racing heart, skipped heartbeats, shaking, sweating, and blushing. In other cases, the symptoms may be milder but last longer. This is often the case when, for example, someone might worry for days, weeks, or even months about attending a wedding.

Another aspect of social phobia is the tendency to *avoid.* Many people with social phobia will avoid situations that make them anxious. Often, though, they can't avoid such situations (or they won't allow themselves to), so they endure the situations with intense anxiety or distress.

Social Phobia: A Hidden Problem of Underestimated Magnitude

It is important for people who suffer from social phobia to know that they are not alone. Far from it! Studies show that at least 1 in 20 people has social phobia. You look around and say, "I don't see that many people who are socially anxious and avoidant! How can that be?" The answer is that social phobia isn't a condition that is easily visible to others. It is not like a broken leg, where people wear casts and use crutches. You look around you and you don't see it. But it's there.

Social anxiety is not a fatal illness, but it can be crippling. Medical researchers talk about *quality of life* to help describe the impact of an illness, and anxiety disorders are known to have a major impact on a person's quality of life. For example, someone with social phobia may be unable to work and socialize with peers. Now, the same may be true for someone with severe heart disease. And while the reasons for the disability may differ—the person with social phobia is too anxious to interact with others and avoids group situations, whereas the person with heart disease is too physically weak to work or leave the house—the reduction in quality of life is similar. When viewed from this perspective, it becomes easier for people who aren't familiar with social anxiety to understand the tremendously negative impact it can have on those who do suffer from it.

Types of Social Anxiety

There are several varieties of social anxiety, differentiated by the kinds of situations that bring it on. For example, many people experience *public speaking anxiety* whether they are proposing a toast at a small dinner party or at a wedding reception of 300 people. Others experience *test anxiety,* where the fear of failing interferes with their ability to study for and perform during the test. *Sports performance anxiety,* where an athlete's fear of performing poorly or making a mistake actually contributes to these feared outcomes, is yet another form of social anxiety. And then there's *dating anxiety,* which is what you'd expect it to be. In fact, so many situations can elicit social anxiety, it would be silly to give them all special names. Instead, researchers have found it useful to classify forms of social anxiety by category.

One of these categories refers to *contingent* and *noncontingent* encounters; for our purposes, we will use the less technical terms *performance* and *interactional. Performance* encounters are those where a person does something in front of others, usually in a rehearsed fashion, and there is no expectation that the person will need to respond to the audience. An example of this would be the class valedictorian who gives a speech at graduation. The speech is written out in advance, and the person's task is to read it with appropriate pauses and intonations. Although the valedictorian may need to respond to the audience—for example, wait for the laughter to subside after a joke before moving on—most of the performance is predetermined.

In contrast, *interactional* social encounters are those where a person must talk, listen, and react appropriately to what others say and do. An example would be someone having a conversation at a party. In this situation, the person needs to initiate a conversation, join in, or respond. He or she then needs to be aware of the other person's responses, and engage in a process of give-and-take that involves attention to verbal and nonverbal cues. In general, interactional social encounters are more demanding, in terms of using more of our mental abilities and social skills, than are performance tasks. Interestingly, however, more people report being afraid of performance encounters such as public speaking than interactional encounters such as conversing at a party.

Here are lists of some social situations commonly feared by people with social anxiety, grouped by whether they are performance or interactional in nature.

Fear of Performance Situations

Performance	Interactional
Public speaking (formal) to large groups	Going to a party
Speaking to small groups	Socializing
Writing in front of others	Making small talk
Eating in front of others	Dating
Entering a room when others are already seated	Asking a teacher for help
Playing a musical instrument	Speaking to a supervisor at work
Playing sports	Asking a salesclerk for help
Using public restrooms	Asking for directions

As you can see, there are many different types of social anxiety. Some people, for example, are unable to write in front of others. Typically, such people will worry that their hands will shake and that others will know they are anxious. They might avoid signing checks in front of other people, or signing charge card slips. This may lead them to either avoid shopping or get someone else to do the shopping for them, or they may choose to pay only with cash. Fear of playing sports because of concerns about looking awkward or foolish are very common, particularly in children and adolescents (more about this in Chap. 4).

Another type of performance anxiety that sounds funny (but isn't if you suffer from it) is the fear of using public restrooms, or *paruresis*. People with paruresis worry that they will be unable to urinate when others are around, or embarrassed if others know they are using the toilet (making the sounds associated with urinating). When they are at home, they have no problem. But when they must use public restrooms, their fear may be so paralyzing that they simply cannot perform.

This may affect men in particular because of the way their restrooms are laid out. At sporting events, for example, men must urinate very quickly while 19 beer-laden guys stand behind them, tapping their feet uncomfortably. For some, this is a very demanding type of performance. Even women, though, who are more likely to have private cubicles in their restrooms, are not immune to paruresis. When paruresis leads to avoidance, people's lives may be restricted by whether they know there is ready access to a "safe" (private) restroom. People with paruresis may choose their jobs on the basis of the layout of the restrooms. They may be unable to travel to new places, or may avoid taking planes or trains. Most of us don't decide whether to go someplace based on the types of restrooms that may or may not be available. But if you're someone who suffers from this problem, it may rule your life.

Fear of Interactional Situations

Interactional anxiety involves situations where a person has to engage in social discourse with at least one other person. A simple interactional situation would be having a conversation with one person, needing to pay attention only to what he or she was saying or doing and responding appropriately. A more complex interactional situation would be having a conversation with several people. Another example of interactional anxiety is fear of dating, a fear closely related to speaking with members of the opposite sex (or, for people who are gay or lesbian, to members of the same sex).

There is also a group of social fears that can be broadly classified as *fear of interacting with people in authority*. For an adult, this might translate into difficulty talking with one's supervisor at work. For children, this might mean being afraid to talk to the teacher.

Then there are interactional fears that involve everyday kinds of social interactions. An example is a man who goes shopping and would prefer to spend 30 minutes looking for a size 36 pair of jeans than ask a salesperson for help. Another example is a woman who would rather drive around for hours than stop and ask for directions. (This behavior occurs in over 90 percent of men, regardless of their level of social anxiety.)

Generalized Social Phobia

Mental health professionals who treat people with social phobia recognize that there are varieties of the disorder, and use a type of clinical shorthand to group those who suffer from it into either the *nongeneralized* or *generalized* type.

People with nongeneralized social phobia usually have one or two performance situations that make them anxious, such as speaking or writing in public. This can be a serious problem for some, but most people with nongeneralized social phobia function well in other types of social situations.

Case History, Nongeneralized Social Phobia: Jennifer

Jennifer, age 26 and single, works in the marketing department of a computer software company. She began as a programmer and was soon promoted to manager, where her people skills and energy drew the attention of the vice president of marketing, who asked her to join his department. Although Jennifer was initially reluctant to leave her comfort zone in programming, she accepted because it was an opportunity to advance her career.

Soon afterward, Jennifer was invited to enroll in an MBA program at the University of California at Irvine. Her supervisor said she was executive material and agreed to pay her tuition and give her time off to attend classes.

Jennifer was terrified. Throughout her education, she had avoided taking classes that would require her to speak in front of others. She readily acknowledged that one of the reasons she had become a programmer in the first place was that the courses involved no public speaking, and grades were based on written work only. The thought of participating in an MBA program—rife with seminars and presentations—was more than Jennifer felt she could handle. She wanted to decline, but knew this would sabotage her career. This is when Jennifer came to us for treatment.

Jennifer has nongeneralized social phobia, in this case limited to public speaking. Although she has struggled with this throughout her life, she has been able to avoid public speaking until now. But now her public speaking anxiety is interfering with her career goals. This is often when people with nongeneralized social phobia seek help—when they can no longer successfully avoid the situations that bring on their anxiety.

Contrast this with people who suffer from generalized social phobia. These people fear a broad array of social situations, usually from both the performance and interactional categories. Yes, they may be unable to speak in front of large groups of people, but that is often the least of their worries. People with generalized social phobia are often uncomfortable in the kinds of social situations that most people take for granted: eating in restaurants, making small talk with colleagues, and attending parties and other social events. People who suffer from generalized social phobia may find that the situations they fear and avoid are so ubiquitous that there are relatively few areas where they function comfortably. It should come as no surprise that this is the most severe form of social phobia.

Case History, Generalized Social Phobia: Kerry

Kerry is 43, divorced, and works as a grade school science teacher. He has a master's degree in electrical engineering, but has not worked in this field for some time. He comes to us for treatment of what he calls his "pathological shyness."

Kerry has been shy for as long as he can remember. He recalls being frightened to speak up in class and having few friends as a youngster. He remembers that he was teased a lot in grade school by his peers, who made fun of his weight (he was a chubby kid) and of his clumsiness ("I had absolutely no talent in sports whatsoever"). He acknowledges that he has been sensitive to criticism throughout his life, and that he still takes even the tiniest slight to heart.

In his teens, Kerry found he was unable to speak to women, despite an intense interest in them. He found himself paralyzed when he had to approach a girl: "I'd freeze, I'd blush, and I couldn't say a word even if a gun had been pointed at my head. Actually, that's what I felt like inside—like a gun had been pointed at me!" He blamed himself for his "weakness," dropped out of high school, and began drinking excessively.

Within a few years, Kerry had become an alcoholic. He continued to live with his mother, but was not working and did little other than drink. To his credit, he was able—after several failed attempts ("My doctor told me to go to Alcoholics Anonymous, and I tried, but there was no way I could speak in front of all those people")—to quit drinking. He went back to school and eventually earned a master's degree. He finally mustered the courage to ask out a fellow student, whom he married after a brief courtship, but he resumed drinking and the marriage soon failed.

When we saw him for treatment, Kerry had been sober for two years. He had obtained his teacher's certificate, and was in his first year of teaching science to fifth- and sixth-graders. He enjoyed the job, and from all accounts was good at it. Yet he found himself unable to interact with the other teachers, who viewed him as distant or snobbish. He had no social life, was back living with his mother, and was terrified that if things didn't improve, he might start drinking again.

Kerry has had problems with severe social anxiety throughout his life. His anxiety is not limited to one or two scenarios. Rather, his social anxiety is pervasive, adversely affecting many areas of his life. Like many people with generalized social phobia, Kerry's symptoms worsened in adolescence, a time when many people become extremely sensitive about the way they are perceived by their peers. Kerry began using alcohol excessively, also a problem that affects many people with social phobia. (We will discuss this further in Chap. 3.) Kerry's generalized social phobia continues to have a profound negative impact on his life.

Am I Too Socially Anxious?

The answer to this question requires that you ask yourself, "Does my social anxiety make me feel nervous or uncomfortable a lot of the time? Does my social anxiety interfere with things I want to do now or in the foreseeable future? Does it prevent me from doing things? Does it keep me from enjoying pleasurable activities? Does it lead to me being alone and lonely?" If you answered *yes* to any of these questions, you may have social phobia.

The good news is that help is available. The purpose of this book is to provide you with information that will enable you to tackle your shyness and social anxiety head-on. You will need a good understanding of what social anxiety looks like and feels like, where it may be coming from, and what other kinds of problems are often associated with it.

These are the topics we cover in the rest of Part One. In Part Two, we focus on self-help, and outline specific techniques and exercises you can use to help yourself overcome shyness and social anxiety. We also cover medication and treatments for children and adolescents in Part Two. In Part Three, we talk about ways to improve your relationships. An epilogue describes the highs and lows you may encounter as you strive to free yourself from social anxiety. Finally, we list a variety of resources you may find useful as you continue the work.

CHAPTER 2

The Origins of Social Anxiety

At this point you may be wondering what makes someone excessively shy. The answer is complex, but (we think) fascinating. There is evidence that shyness and excessive social anxiety are based in biology. But learning and experience also contribute. In this chapter, we will review some exciting research about the origins of social anxiety, emphasizing what we do and do not know.

What Have We Learned from Monkeys?

We can learn a lot from watching animals. Just last month, one of us spent a week watching dogs at play and learned to fetch. (We also learned of a somewhat unorthodox—for humans—use of trees, but that's better left alone. Stay tuned for our next book, *Overcoming Your Fear of Vegetation.*) Some scientists (apparently with a lot of time on their hands, or with tenure) spend weeks and months watching nonhuman primates (for instance, baboons) in their natural habitats, with the goal of learning about their behavior. They believe that by studying the actions of nonhuman primates, they will learn about some of the factors that govern the way we behave. (In this section, we use the terms *monkey, baboon, ape, chimpanzee, nonhuman primate,* and *Volvo* interchangeably, belying our inability to tell most of these creatures apart. We hope that animal lovers, zoologists, and those of you who actually conduct this research will forgive us this imprecision.)

Monkeys are more like humans than many of us care to acknowledge. They live in families, care for their young, and interact in very sophisticated ways that reveal a complex underlying social structure (sometimes referred to as a social *hierarchy*). They live in groups where one monkey becomes the boss and the others have specific, well-defined roles. There are different rules for baby monkeys, adolescents and adults. Sound familiar? The fact that monkeys develop a sophisticated social structure suggests that there are innate biological factors driving these behaviors. We therefore believe that these factors must also be operative, to a greater or lesser extent, in the most evolved primates, human beings.

We have learned from studying nonhuman primates that some behaviors are biologically determined. Shyness is a good example. Some baby monkeys are inquisitive and daring, while others are inhibited and timid. These tendencies, which show themselves early in life, are strongly determined by genes, and probably less so by the environment. This is not to say, however, that genes alone determine shyness (or any other trait). Nor does it suggest that if you're born with "shy genes" you are destined to be a shy person for the remainder of your days. Nothing in life is that simple.

Baboons. These are fairly large nonhuman primates that Robert Sapolsky, a renowned researcher at Stanford University, studies in the wilds of a tropical island jungle. Although this may sound like an excellent scheme for writing off one's vacation, Sapolsky is a serious scientist (who, we must admit, seems to enjoy his work just a little bit more than anyone has a right to) with an interest in the neurobiology of stress. He has found, through years of painstaking work in the field, that baboons smell bad. More important (not if you're sitting next to one, however), baboons have a social hierarchy where one male is the boss (or *dominant*), and others are *subordinate;* they stay away from him and exhibit submissive behaviors that let the boss know he's in charge. These behaviors include not looking directly at the head honcho baboon (it is considered very bad form in most animal societies to stare directly into another animal's eyes), keeping the head down when the chief baboon is in the vicinity, and letting the dominant animal have first access to food and water. Sapolsky has shown that the submissive animals have very high levels of cortisol, a stress hormone, in their blood. This goes to show that, in the words of Mel Brooks, "It's good to be king." It is unclear whether having a high level of cortisol leads certain baboons to become submissive, or whether the stress of being submissive results in the high cortisol levels (Sapolsky suspects the latter is the case). This important work does, however, raise the question of whether social anxiety in humans is similar to social submissiveness in nonhuman primates.

Surprisingly, shyness isn't just something we see in complex creatures like monkeys. We can even see it in fish.

Who Gets the Girl? Shy and Bold Guppies

Lee Dugatkin, a researcher at the University of Louisville, studies the behavior of guppies. The guppy behavior with which we are most familiar from caring for our children's pets is the one where the guppy lies on its back and floats. But Dugatkin, who is obviously more adept at caring for fish than we are, gets his guppies to participate in some fascinating experiments.

Some guppies are *bold* and some guppies are *timid*. A bold guppy is one who will swim up to a big predator fish, stare it in the face, and risk getting eaten. A timid guppy will hang out in the background and watch the predator fish from afar. Dugatkin and his students conduct experiments where they put guppies into tanks, then add a plastic predator fish and watch what happens. They have learned that the behavior of particular guppies is very predictable. If you're a bold guppy one day, you're a bold guppy the next day. And vice versa—if you're a timid guppy today, you're timid tomorrow, too. Furthermore, they found that bold guppies are more likely to be brightly colored (usually orange) than their timid confreres. It's almost as if the bold guppies are saying to the predator fish, "Here I am. Come and get me!" This doesn't sound like a good way to promote one's survival, does it?

As it turns out, bold (orange) boy guppies are more likely to get the girl than timid (white or gray) ones. That is, female guppies are more interested in mating with the bright orange males. This startling observation led to some remarkable occurrences. First, we have it on good authority that all the male students in Dugatkin's lab showed up the next day with orange hair. Second, it got Dugatkin thinking about the pros and cons of being bold or timid. He concluded that being bold (if you're a guppy) increases both your chances of procreating and the likelihood that you will be eaten by a predator. Being timid decreases your chances of procreating, but also decreases your chances of being eaten. Timid guppies may therefore have a longer lifetime during which to mate. What does this tell us about the value of being bold or timid if you happen to be human?

Well, possibly nothing, but it's hard to resist a good fish story. The point of the story, now that we're forced to come up with one, is that if fish can be shy, then shyness must be a pretty basic behavior, one that doesn't require a lot of thinking or reasoning or learning. In the case of guppies, being timid or shy is almost certainly an inborn behavior—mommy and daddy guppies don't teach it to their kids. Might this also be the case for human beings?

The Biology of Social Attachment

Let's move away from monkeys and fish and talk about a species nearer and dearer to our hearts, the prairie vole. What, you might ask, is a prairie vole? Neither of us has ever encountered a prairie vole, despite having spent most of our lives living on the prairie. But Tom Insel, a distinguished neuroscientist at Emory University, tells us that a prairie vole is a very social little rodent. Male prairie voles are monogamous. (Our editor tells us that using *monogamous* as a descriptor for *male* is an oxymoron. Fortunately, our feelings are not easily hurt.) A closely related creature, the montane vole, lacks the family values of the Midwest prairie vole and fails to establish the same kinds of close and enduring social relationships. It apparently hangs out in the vole equivalent of singles bars and leaves a trail of little broken vole hearts in its wake. These two species of rodents are genetically very similar, though their brains differ slightly in their secretion patterns of a particular hormone—vasopressin. Vasopressin (and a related hormone, oxytocin) seem to play an important role in determining the extent to which these animals make and maintain social attachments. Researchers believe that these hormones may be important determinants of behavior in humans, too.

Inhibited Children . . . Socially Anxious Adults

Parents and relatives are often struck by how different young children in the same family can be, beginning very early in life. Some children are easily upset and frightened, whereas others rarely cry and are less easily frightened. Some children sleep a great deal early in life, and others are wide awake and alert much of the time. Some children love to explore and try new things, and others are cautious and bothered by change. We call these characteristics, present from very early in life, *temperament*. Most of us have heard stories from our parents about our childhood temperaments, something most of us cannot clearly remember ourselves. Sometimes these stories define us, even as adults.

Renowned developmental psychologist Jerome Kagan and his colleagues at Harvard University have for the past decade and a half been studying *behaviorally inhibited* children. By inhibited, they mean children who, from an early age, are slow to warm up in the presence of strangers and timid about exploring new environments. About 15 to 20 percent of the children Kagan studied had this form of behavior at 3 years of age. In a series of important studies, Kagan's group has shown that the most inhibited of these children tend to stay this way as they grow older. This is not to say that *all* children who are behaviorally inhibited at 3 grow up to become socially phobic adults. The relationship is not nearly that clear. In fact, many behaviorally inhibited children in the studies did outgrow it by the time they reached 7 years of age. (Some of these children may have benefited from their parents' efforts to help them overcome their behavioral inhibition; we'll talk more about this later in this book.) But very inhibited children are three to four times as likely as less inhibited children to become anxious adults.

Behaviorally inhibited children are also more likely to have a parent with social anxiety disorder, suggesting that the conditions are related. It has also been shown that social anxiety disorder, particularly the generalized type, tends to run in families.

How might we explain these findings? It is possible, of course, that parents with social anxiety disorder behave in ways that lead their children to be inhibited. For example, a child might see his father avoid talking to new people, or refuse to answer the phone. The child might get the message that these situations are frightening or dangerous, and might therefore begin to fear them. In addition, socially anxious parents might attempt to protect their child from the experiences that they recall made them anxious when they were young. For example, if a socially anxious mother sees her son begin to cry when left with other children, she might rescue the child by taking him in her arms, rather than encourage him to stay in the situation and learn to cope. So it may be that behaviorally inhibited children learn these patterns from socially anxious adults. But social anxiety might also be transmitted genetically.

Anxious Genes?

If we look at identical twins, whose genes are 100 percent similar, we find that levels of shyness (and social anxiety) are fairly similar—more so than in nonidentical (fraternal) twins, whose genes are 50 percent similar (the same as nontwin siblings). This leads us to conclude that genes influence a person's tendency to be socially anxious. Probably many genes (rather than a single "shyness" gene), each of which contributes a little to one's personality, influence a person's level of shyness or social anxiety. Investigators around the world are searching for these genes.

We remind you that we do not suggest that genes are the *only* things that determine whether a person will be socially anxious. Experiences both early and later in life, as well as family environment, also shape people's personalities beyond the influence of their genes. But genetic makeup forms the basic template for personality (including the tendency to be shy), and this may affect the way we experience the world as we grow up. These experiences may, in turn, influence the way our biological systems (including the brain) develop, and therein the ways we view and interact with the world.

But genes and biology are not destiny. Many conditions are strongly influenced but not ultimately determined by genetic factors. Examples include diabetes and heart disease. If you inherit "bad" insulin genes or "bad" cholesterol genes from your parents, you can modify your behavior— change your diet, exercise regularly—to increase your chances of staying healthy. If this is true for conditions such as diabetes and heart disease, it must be equally true—if not more so—for social anxiety disorder. Some of us may inherit more than our fair share of "shyness" genes. This doesn't mean that disabling social anxiety will paralyze us. Human beings have the option of choosing to change the way they experience their lives. You can adopt a new world view. You can get rid of old habits. Anxious genes or not—you *can* overcome social anxiety.

Growing-Up Years and Social Anxiety

The people who influence us when we are children have a profound impact on our development. Whether we like it or not, our parents, our siblings, our teachers, and our friends all play a part in determining who we become.

Some people with social anxiety come from healthy, supportive families. But when we look at a large number of people with serious social anxiety, we find that many more of them have troubled family backgrounds than do people without anxiety. It is worthwhile to consider how your family background may have helped or hindered the development of your confidence in social situations.

Stories of Family Experiences

Janice: "My father was an alcoholic."

Janice is a 33-year-old checkout clerk at a large supermarket who has had problems with social anxiety and depression since her midteens. She recalls seeing her father, an appliance salesman, come home drunk many nights. She says that her father was a "happy" drunk. He didn't scream at or hit Janice or her mother. But he spoke loudly and was often drunk when they were out in public, and Janice remembers being ashamed of him. As a teenager, she worried that other kids would see her father when he was drunk (which was much of the time). She discouraged her father from attending school functions and never brought friends home from school.

Janice believes her father's alcoholism was an important factor in her development of social anxiety disorder. She thinks her father's drinking made her fearful of being around other people. She also believes that her desire to keep others away from her father led her to lose friends, a problem that got worse as she got older.

More than 10 years ago, Janice saw a therapist who specialized in treating adult children of alcoholics. Janice stopped therapy after a year, feeling she had made a lot of progress working through the anger she harbored toward her father, as well as toward her mother, whom she felt should have done something to make her dad stop drinking. Janice's parents are divorced, and though she still sees her mother regularly, she rarely sees or speaks to her father. She continues to experience problems with social anxiety.

Many people with social anxiety report that one or both of their parents had a drinking problem. Janice believes her father's alcoholism contributed to her becoming socially anxious, and she might be right. Janice found it useful to talk with a therapist about her relationship with her father. It helped her let go of some of the resentment she felt toward him, but this didn't help her cope with her social anxiety. Gaining insight into the origins of a social anxiety problem is, in our experience, rarely sufficient to make the problem go away. More often than not, overcoming social anxiety requires an active approach—the kind you'll be learning about in this book.

By the same token, you don't have to resolve childhood conflicts with your parents in order to overcome social phobia. Sometimes these conflicts run very deep and cannot be resolved. This doesn't mean that you can't directly tackle your shyness. You can. Resolving longstanding conflicts with parents can be gratifying, but if you can't do it, or you choose not to, this will not interfere with your ability to overcome your social anxiety. Furthermore, if you feel that your social anxiety is *the* major problem in your life right now, we recommend that you focus on it right now—and leave other matters for later. Nobody is without emotional baggage. You don't need to unload it all to deal with social anxiety!

Karen: "My mom was a nervous wreck."

Karen is a 54-year-old schoolteacher with social anxiety disorder. She grew up in a single-parent family, never having known her father. She remembers being a fearful child, afraid to leave her mother's side. She cried when she had to attend kindergarten, and her mother had to stay in the classroom with her for the first two weeks.

Karen's mother was a shy, introverted woman with few friends. She had been hospitalized for a nervous breakdown immediately after Karen's birth, and Karen was cared for primarily by her grandmother during the first year of her life. Her early memories of her mother are of a frightened, unhappy woman who kept to herself. Karen rarely had the opportunity to play with other children in her preschool years; she recalls being lonely for most of her childhood.

Karen's mother experienced repeated episodes of severe depression, some of which resulted in additional periods of hospitalization. When her mother was in the hospital, Karen again moved in with her grandmother, who lived in another part of town. This necessitated switching schools several times during elementary and middle school, sometimes in the middle of the year. Karen recalls how hard this was for her, being separated from friends and needing to establish new relationships time and time again. After a while, she says, she just gave up and became a loner. She also remembers being embarrassed about not having a father and "having a crazy mother."

It is not unusual for someone with social anxiety to have a parent or a sibling with depression or anxiety. These problems tend to run in families and are believed to have a genetic basis. Karen may have inherited some of these genes from her mother, but it is clear that her mother's mental illness affected her in other ways. She was separated from her mother early in life because of her mother's hospitalization, and was deprived of the opportunity to socialize with other children when she was very young. The circumstances of her mother's illness later forced her to change schools repeatedly—a difficult thing for a child to do, especially when she is shy to begin with.

Knowing all these things helps Karen understand how her experiences have shaped her; they are part of her personal story. But knowing this story is not enough to enable Karen to overcome her social anxiety. That requires special work, as you'll learn later in this book.

People sometimes tell us about other kinds of family difficulties that they feel may have contributed to their social anxiety. These include growing up in families where the following conditions are typical:

♦ There is a lot of conflict between adults.

♦ The adults are overly critical of the children and nothing is ever good enough.

♦ There is excessive concern about what other people think.

We hear these stories frequently enough to make us believe that it is possible that having these childhood experiences makes it more likely that a person will experience social anxiety later in life. On the other hand, it is important to realize that many people have these kinds of experiences and *don't* develop social anxiety. It may be that people who are genetically prone to social anxiety are sensitive to these kinds of experiences. A very extroverted, gregarious child may find it easy to brush off negative comments from an overcritical parent. But a timid, introspective child may be more likely to take these comments to heart, leading to greater insecurity and self-doubt.

If you're a parent, you must be wondering if there is anything you can do that *won't* lead your child to resent you later in life. Of course there is. If you can leave a large inheritance, that can be very helpful. But, short of that, there are no guarantees. Take solace, though, in the knowledge that if you've been an adequate parent—and most of us are—and your child is having difficulty with anxiety, it is typically *not* something you have caused.

Beyond Parenting

Research has recently shown that the effects of parenting may have been overestimated. Our parents and other family members have undoubtedly contributed to our development in many subtle (and some not so subtle) ways. But studies are revealing that we are also shaped to a great extent by the experiences we have with people outside the family: with teachers, with coaches, and most of all, with peers.

Thomas: "Kids say the meanest things."

Thomas is a 28-year-old securities account clerk with a midsized brokerage firm. His social anxiety has hampered his career advancement (most employees his age have been promoted to management positions). Thomas is single and has never been in a long-term romantic relationship.

He remembers his social anxiety starting when he was 14 and a sophomore in high school. He was short for his age and slow to mature physically. He dreaded gym class because it showcased his lack of athletic skills and because he felt like a little boy among young men and women.

The other kids (especially the girls) teased Thomas mercilessly, and the more they laughed, the more he blushed and tried to hide. He dreaded making eye contact for fear that someone would say something nasty to him. In his junior and senior years, he was pushed around by some of the school tough guys, usually in the presence of their girlfriends. He recalls high school as being pure hell.

Thomas's experiences in high school had a devastating impact on his self-esteem, and undoubtedly contributed to the social anxiety that now plagues him. It has been very important for him to understand that although teenagers are often cruel, most of us outgrow this nastiness. This realization has helped Thomas approach his adult relationships with a different set of expectations. He no longer expects every social encounter to lead to embarrassment, nor does he believe that most people he talks to want to make him feel like a fool. Knowing this is helping Thomas relate to adults differently, and to get unstuck from high school mode. He has to practice this new way of relating, though, because it doesn't come naturally to him.

Getting Over Growing Up

Old habits, particularly old ways of thinking, die hard. While understanding where these habits and thinking patterns come from can be helpful, mere understanding isn't enough. Nor is it always necessary—sometimes you just can't figure it out. And blaming people—parents, teachers, siblings, or peers—for how you've turned out will not lead to changes in yourself. In order to tackle social anxiety, you need to learn new ways of relating to people, new ways of behaving around others, and new ways of thinking about social situations. And once you've learned these things, you need to practice them again and again.

CHAPTER 3

The Company That Social Anxiety Keeps

Social anxiety frequently travels in the company of other emotional difficulties. These include marital problems, depression, alcohol or drug abuse, and other anxiety disorders.

Marital and Relationship Problems

Tamara: "I think he's going to leave me."

Tamara is 32 years old, the mother of two boys, ages 12 and 10, and works as a homemaker. She is married to Mark, age 34, an outgoing, amicable real estate sales agent. Tamara fears her marriage is on rocky ground.

Tamara has had social anxiety disorder since age 13. She remembers feeling very self-conscious when she began to grow tall and develop physically. By the time she was 14, she looked like an 18-year-old. Everyone, including her parents, told her she was beautiful, and she acknowledges this was probably true, but says she felt like a freak. Older boys were attracted to her, but her parents wouldn't let her date until she was 16. Prior to that, she did very little socializing, avoiding the company of all but her closest friends.

Shortly after she turned 16, Mark, a high school senior and "all-around jock," invited her to a dance. Their relationship bloomed: "He made me feel comfortable. I could go out with him, he'd put his arm around my shoulder, and I felt safe. I didn't need to speak to anyone; he'd answer for me. I could just smile and look pretty." They were married when Tamara was 19 and Mark was 21. Mark was in college; Tamara completed high school and lived at home until she was married.

The 13 years of her marriage were a blur. Tamara raised the children while Mark established himself professionally. She had a few close friends from high school, and became friendly with the mothers of some of her children's classmates. Because of her social anxiety, Tamara didn't get involved with the usual school and church kinds of things that stay-at-home moms took part in. Tamara felt lonely and isolated much of the time. She had difficulty confiding in others except for Mark, but work took up most of his time. She attended business functions with her husband, "on his arm, looking pretty as always," but felt inferior to the other spouses, most of whom had college degrees or business interests of their own. She found it increasingly difficult to participate in conversations at social events, and soon reached the point where she said very little about anything. This led to arguments with Mark, who insisted she was being unreasonable in worrying too much about the opinions of others.

Now Tamara feared that her marriage was in trouble, but she dared not raise the issue with Mark and would not consider asking him to join her in counseling. She felt dependent on him financially and emotionally, and couldn't imagine fending for herself without him. She admitted that her marriage had not been good in a long time, but felt that the alternative—raising the children alone, and perhaps dating and establishing another relationship in the future—was too terrifying even to consider. She felt trapped.

Some people with social anxiety have had limited dating experience prior to entering their first long-term relationship. In fact, it is not unusual for people with social anxiety to marry after dating only one or two people. We have heard people with social anxiety say things like, "I couldn't believe any woman would be interested in me. When I found out she was, I didn't want to risk losing her. So we got married." Or, "The idea of dating, of having to meet and talk to new people until I found Mr. Right was just too scary. I wasn't in love with him, but I was comfortable."

This works for some people. We have seen some wonderful marriages where the motivation to marry may have been a form of avoidance, but the couple developed a strong, healthy relationship nonetheless. But just as often, we have seen this kind of union dissolve. This often happens when the children get older and the socially anxious partner finds he or she still feels alone, despite being married. Or marital problems can erupt when someone with social anxiety gets treatment and begins to blossom, and the spouse can't handle this newfound independence—an independence that can drastically change the balance of power in a relationship (usually for the better!).

Depression

Rick: "I thought I was losing my mind."

Rick is a tall, 28-year-old college graduate working as a computer graphics programmer. He is not presently in a relationship. He dates occasionally, but finds it difficult to speak to women. He is satisfied with his job, though he notes that he has turned down two promotions: "I couldn't talk in front of groups. It would have been impossible."

Rick was a shy kid whose parents had to literally push him through the kindergarten door. He nonetheless did well in school, earning good grades and an acceptance to college. In his freshman year, away from home for the first time and without friends, he suffered a nervous breakdown. Things got so bad that Rick thought about killing himself. He began weekly sessions with a counselor in the student mental health service, who helped get him through the crisis. He went home for winter break, felt a lot better, and managed to complete the year.

The following year, Rick again began to feel like he was losing it. He went back to the counselor, who recommended that he see a psychiatrist who would prescribe an antidepressant. Rick was resistant, preferring to handle it on his own. But after several more weeks of "crying like a baby," in his words, and finding it nearly impossible to get out of bed, Rick went to see the school psychiatrist, who started him on an antidepressant. Though he felt some nausea for the first few days, Rick found that he began to feel better about three weeks into treatment; in his words, "The fog began to lift." He stayed on the antidepressant throughout college, and the depression did not recur.

Emotional problems often travel in packs. Among sufferers of social anxiety disorder, about one in three also experiences difficulties with *major depression*. In particular, those people whose social anxiety starts early in life seem to have the most problems with depression. We don't know for sure why so many people with social anxiety disorder get depressed. It may be that whatever genes increase the risk for social anxiety also increase the risk for depression. Or it may be, at least for some people, that the frustrations and limitations imposed by social anxiety lead them to become depressed. It is also possible that the loneliness and isolation that so often accompany social anxiety leave the person with few social supports, and therefore more vulnerable to depression.

Although we don't always understand why some people with social anxiety get depressed, we do know that it happens frequently—often enough that you should be on the lookout for it. Signs and symptoms of major depression include the following:

- ♦ Loss of interest in activities
- ♦ Feeling sad, down, blue, unhappy
- ♦ Sleep problems (too much or too little)
- ♦ Appetite problems (too much or too little)
- ♦ Inability to concentrate
- ♦ Feelings of helplessness or hopelessness
- ♦ Low energy
- ♦ Inability to experience pleasure
- ♦ Blaming yourself for your situation
- ♦ Feeling life isn't worth living (or even thinking about ending it)

If you find yourself experiencing several of these symptoms for more than two weeks, chances are you are suffering from major depression. There are some good self-help books to help you deal with the depression (see the resources section). There is also a growing interest in herbal remedies such as St. John's wort. If your depression isn't disabling, you may want to consider some of these approaches before you seek professional help. But if you're not getting better in a relatively short period of time (a month or two at most), or if you're feeling worse, or if you are having any thoughts of commiting suicide or harming someone else, you should immediately seek treatment from a physician or other mental health professional.

Another condition often experienced by people with social anxiety disorder is *dysthymia*. Dysthymia is a chronic form of depression that is less intense than major depression. People with dysthymia report feeling down, blue, or disinterested nearly every day for a very long time—typically many years. They may also experience episodes of major depression lasting several months, but even when they recover from these more severe episodes, they don't feel well.

Fortunately, many approaches used to treat social anxiety disorder also work for major depression and dysthymia. Antidepressants are the primary medications used to treat social anxiety disorder, and some of the psychological treatments used for shyness and social anxiety also work for depression. We'll talk more about this later when we discuss treatments.

Excessive Use of Alcohol or Drugs

Many people find that alcohol reduces anxiety. It is not unusual for someone to have a few drinks to become more comfortable at a social event; as we mentioned earlier, some people have a few drinks before the event even starts. Despite some temporary reduction of symptoms, however, using alcohol to relieve anxiety can lead to alcohol abuse. While alcohol's immediate effect is often to reduce anxiety, later that day or the next it can produce feelings of increased anxiety, irritability, or depression. This can happen even at moderate levels of social drinking. The person may not consume enough to experience a hangover, but mood and anxiety may still be affected. The person may not notice this pattern because the sick feelings that accompany a hangover may be mild, or even absent.

One warning level that has been established is regular consumption of five or more alcoholic drinks in a day. This level of consumption puts you at risk of motor vehicle accidents, interpersonal problems, and needing increasing amounts of alcohol over time to produce the desired relaxation effect. We *strongly* encourage people to limit their alcohol intake to one or two drinks at a social occasion and to avoid using alcohol to reduce anxiety. We are adamant about this because one in five people with social anxiety disorder develops alcohol or drug problems. Are you one of these people? Take the test in Fig. 3.1.

If you think you are using alcohol excessively, you should do something about it. If heavy alcohol use has become a part of your routine, you are likely to find it tough to stop drinking on your own. There are many excellent organizations whose mission is to help people quit drinking and regain control of their lives. The best known, of course, is Alcoholics Anonymous (AA). There are AA groups in virtually every city, town, and

Think about the *past year* and answer *yes* or *no* to each of the following questions:

♦ Do you have a drink containing alcohol four or more times a week?

♦ On a typical day when you are drinking, do you have five or more drinks containing alcohol?

♦ Have there been times when you were not able to stop drinking once you started?

♦ Have there been times when you needed a drink in the morning to get yourself going?

♦ Have you had a feeling of guilt or remorse after drinking?

♦ Has someone close to you (relative, friend, coworker, or doctor) been concerned about your drinking or suggested you cut down?

If you answered *yes* to more than one of these questions, you may have a drinking problem and should strongly consider seeking help!

Figure 3.1   Self-test on alcohol consumption.

hole-in-the-wall in the United States, Canada, and around the world. You can also seek help from mental health counselors (if you are still in school); from your church, synagogue, mosque, or other religious organization; and from employee health organizations. The bottom line is, if you're motivated to deal with your drinking problem, there is a group out there eager to help you accomplish your goal.

If you have a drinking problem, it is wise to try to tackle it before you invest much effort in dealing with social anxiety. The reason is simple: if you're still drinking, particularly as a crutch to cope with anxiety, you're unlikely to get better until you can give it up.

What do you do, though, if you feel that you can't tackle your drinking problem until your social anxiety is at least somewhat better? We know people who say that they tried to go to AA but were so anxious around other people that they couldn't even stay in the room. What should you do if you're in this boat?

If you have tried to join a supervised alcohol treatment program like AA but find that your social anxiety prevents you from participating, you need professional help. Find a doctor or therapist with experience in treating anxiety disorders. This is not always an easy thing to do—you should find the resources section of this book helpful. Your therapist should be able to help you get a handle on both the drinking and the anxiety (this might involve medication), so you can participate in an alcohol treatment program. Once the drinking is under control, you can focus on conquering your social anxiety.

If you are using street drugs—and this includes marijuana—or abusing prescription medications (taking more than prescribed, or using medications prescribed for someone else) you must tackle this problem early on, as it will be very difficult (or impossible) to overcome your social anxiety if you are abusing drugs. There are services available in nearly every community to help you overcome your drug abuse problem. Take advantage of them.

Anxiety Disorders and Related Conditions

People with social anxiety sometimes have problems with other kinds of anxiety. Again, this is because these kinds of problems tend to cluster (the medical term for this is *comorbidity*). Here are some examples:

Generalized Anxiety Disorder

Generalized anxiety disorder involves excessive, chronic worrying about life in general—health, finances, work, children—just about anything. Worry is not limited to social situations. At least one in five people with social anxiety disorder also has generalized anxiety disorder.

Panic Disorder

You begin to feel tense and short of breath. Your heart starts to race and pound in your chest. You feel dizzy, and things begin to feel unreal around you. You are sweating but at the same time feel cold and shaky. You have a strong desire to flee. If you have these symptoms, you may be having a *panic attack.*

While people with social anxiety disorder may have panic attacks during socially threatening situations or when they worry about them in advance, there are others whose panic attacks come totally out of the blue, unrelated to a recognizable situation or worry. In some cases, panic attacks can even awaken people from sleep. When these attacks occur repeatedly, we say the

person suffers from *panic disorder*. Sometimes it is difficult for the person—
or even an experienced therapist—to distinguish between panic disorder
(and its close cousin, *agoraphobia*) and social anxiety disorder. A key difference is that people with social anxiety disorder will, in the midst of an
anxiety attack, be thinking about how they appear to others, and worrying
about embarrassing themselves. In contrast, people with panic disorder
will typically be worrying about the physical symptoms, wondering if they
are having a heart attack or a stroke. But sometimes it's not so clear. If
you're uncertain whether you're experiencing panic disorder or social anxiety disorder, consult an experienced mental health professional.

Other Anxiety Disorders

Persons suffering from social phobia may experience still other forms of
anxiety. These include specific phobias (fear of flying, fear of spiders, fear
of heights, to name a few); obsessive-compulsive disorder, characterized by
unwanted intrusive thoughts and the need to perform actions repeatedly
(for example, a fear of contamination accompanied by a need to wash
repeatedly); and posttraumatic stress disorder (recurring memories, anxiety, irritability, and sleep problems that begin after a traumatic event such
as a rape, mugging, or serious car accident). We don't have room to discuss
each of these here, but encourage you to get more information by referring
to the resources section.

Body Dysmorphic Disorder

Body dysmorphic disorder (*BDD*) has been referred to as the disorder of
imagined ugliness. People with BDD typically believe something is wrong
with some part of their bodies. For example, someone with BDD might
believe his or her nose is too large or misshapen, and avoid other people
because he or she doesn't want them to see it. Research shows there may be
a relationship between some forms of social anxiety and BDD. If you spend
a great deal of time worrying about some aspect of your appearance, you
may be suffering from BDD and should seek professional help.

Medical Problems

Any medical problem that is visible to others may be associated with social
anxiety. For example, a woman who stutters may be self-conscious and
avoid speaking around other people. A man with Parkinson's disease (a
neurological disorder that causes shaking and trembling—boxer Muham-

mad Ali and actor Michael J. Fox have this illness) may grow self-conscious and avoid interacting with other people. Sometimes, a person's avoidance of social situations can reach proportions where it significantly interferes with his or her ability to function. In these cases, although social anxiety disorder may not be formally diagnosed, treating the social anxiety symptoms can improve a person's overall quality of life. So, if you have a medical condition that is visible to others (additional examples include obesity, acne, scarring from burns or accidents, birthmarks, or birth defects) and find you are avoiding people because you are embarrassed by your appearance, you will benefit from reading this book.

A Good Place to Start

Working to overcome shyness and social anxiety will improve your health in many ways. First, you will feel less stressed, and second, you will develop friendships and maintain social relationships more easily. Studies show that people who experience less stress and have more social supports tend to maintain better overall health. So do yourself a favor. Invest some time and energy to tackle your social anxiety. It will help you in ways you couldn't have imagined.

CHAPTER 4

You're Never
Too Young

Severe shyness and social anxiety occur in children as well as adults. Remember, many adults with social phobia say their problems began when they were much younger. Often, though, they are not recognized as problems by teachers, counselors, coaches or, sometimes, even parents. In this chapter we'll describe the kinds of shyness problems kids can have, how to recognize them, and when to be concerned.

When children are very young, shyness is often viewed as an endearing trait, as in, "Look how shy she is, hiding her head in Mommy's shirt. Isn't that cute?" When children are of preschool age, it is common for them to exhibit shyness behaviors such as stranger anxiety (hiding, crying, or running to Mommy when a new person enters the room), remaining very quiet around people with whom they are not familiar, or clinging to Daddy when in a novel situation. These kinds of behaviors are not, within reason, abnormal in a preschooler. They are, however, very much abnormal in a fifth-grader.

One of the difficulties we experience as parents is knowing when a child has moved from "that's normal" terrain to "this just ain't right" territory. What is developmentally appropriate for a 3-year-old is rarely appropriate for an 11-year-old. But since we are so close to our children and see them develop over a long period of time, parents are often not great at detecting abnormalities in their kids. Parents typically know when their children are very anxious, but tend to rate them as less anxious than the children rate themselves. What is the explanation for this phenomenon?

The truth is that we are too busy making lunches and driving carpool to notice much of what's going on in the emotional lives of our kids. We're not talking about bad parents; we're talking about very, very good parents. Emotions are felt strongly, but they are internal states: unless someone tells you that he or she is anxious or uncomfortable, it can be very hard to know. Children will sometimes tell us, though they don't always have the words to say it in a way that makes sense to adults. Teenagers, of course, prefer to tell us nothing.

Physical Symptoms

Children under age 8 or 9 are more likely to mention they are experiencing physical symptoms than say they are anxious or afraid. Some physical symptoms that socially anxious children experience are the following:

♦ Stomach aches

♦ Queasiness or butterflies in stomach

♦ Nausea

♦ Rapid heartbeat

♦ Shortness of breath

♦ Dizziness

♦ Dry mouth

♦ Blushing

♦ Headaches

If your child describes these symptoms in relation to social situations, the problem may be social anxiety. For example, if your son says he has a stomach ache before he has to go to school in the morning, then social anxiety is a possible (but not the only) culprit. Or, if a child says she's dizzy when she needs to present an oral report in class, the teacher should suspect social anxiety.

Actions Speak Louder than Words

Are there other ways to know if your child is having a problem with anxiety? Yes, you can often infer from people's *behavior* that they are anxious, uncomfortable, or upset. In the case of social anxiety, you can learn a lot by paying attention to what your child *avoids*. What kinds of situations do kids with social anxiety try to avoid?

+ Speaking in class
+ Making presentations
+ Reading aloud
+ Taking tests
+ Writing on the board
+ Eating in front of others
+ Inviting kids over to play
+ Going to parties
+ Playing sports

If your child is avoiding doing some of these things, he or she may be experiencing social anxiety. How do you know for sure? Start by asking your child about it: "I've noticed you haven't wanted to go to some of the birthday parties of kids in your class. The parties sound like a lot of fun. Is there some reason you don't want to go? Is there something you're worried about?" You can follow up with, "Sometimes kids worry that they're going to look silly, or that they might say something stupid, or that the other kids won't like them. Are you worrying about any of those things?" You can also talk with your child's teacher to learn whether he or she is interacting with other children in group situations, speaking up in class, and so on.

Selective Mutism

This is a form of social anxiety that affects some young children. Whereas it is perfectly normal for a 4- or 5-year-old to be reluctant to speak in the presence of strangers, particularly adults, it is not normal for a child to say *absolutely nothing* over a prolonged time. We are not referring here to children whose speech or language development is delayed. We are referring to children who speak well (and sometimes a lot!) around their parents and siblings and maybe a close friend or two, but who then are silent around others. When this occurs, it is called *selective mutism*.

Jenna: "Such a sweet (quiet) little girl!"

Jenna is 6 years old and midway through first grade, but has not said a single word to her teacher, Ms. Tompkins, since arriving at school. For the first few weeks, Ms. Tompkins wasn't concerned: Jenna was smiling and nodding a lot, and apparently understood what was being said to her. She sat quietly in class and didn't cause problems. Ms. Tompkins tried to get Jenna to speak to her, but Jenna would just nod her head and smile or frown. Ms. Tompkins was impressed with how well Jenna communicated without words, but was concerned about her lack of speech. She observed Jenna at recess and noticed that she tended to stand on the periphery of the clusters of kids, looking as if she wanted to participate in their games but rarely joining in. As far as Ms. Tompkins could tell, Jenna didn't speak to any of her classmates.

Ms. Tompkins arranged for the school counselor to assess Jenna. The counselor had no more success than Ms. Tompkins in getting Jenna to speak, and decided to bring in Jenna's parents. They told the counselor that Jenna was always a very shy, sensitive, but happy little girl. Because of her shyness, they had not enrolled her in kindergarten, so this was Jenna's first year in a classroom. They were surprised to learn, though, that she had been completely mute since arriving at school. They informed Ms. Tompkins that Jenna "never shut up" at home. In fact, they reported that Jenna came home from school every day and regaled her parents with a report of what she did at school, whom she had played with, and how much fun she was having.

Jenna's mother mentioned that she herself had been a shy child, and also had been extremely quiet at school for the first few years. Even now, she thought of herself as painfully shy, and had in fact struggled with her shyness throughout her life. She was eager to ensure that Jenna did not suffer the same fate.

Children often rely on others to speak for them and make their wishes known. (True, some of us do hire attorneys for that purpose, but we digress. . . .) When they are well behaved—particularly if they are girls—we are often willing to let them remain silent and do the speaking for them. Jenna's selective mutism probably originated from a combination of genetic and learned factors. Given her family history of extreme shyness, she probably inherited a temperament that predisposed her to be socially anxious. This genetic predisposition was then coupled with parents who—with the best of intentions—tried to protect their daughter by enabling her to avoid talking and mingling with other children. Their decision to have Jenna skip kindergarten is an example of how they inadvertently deprived Jenna of an early opportunity to overcome her fears. Fortunately, the problem was detected early, and the school counselor worked with Jenna and her parents to help her tackle it. (We have seen cases where children remain selectively mute for years without receiving any treatment.)

School Phobia

When children start school, they are often anxious when they must separate from their parents. But when a child continues to have trouble separating after several days of trying, further attention may be warranted. Many children experience *separation anxiety;* almost all of them get over it. But 2 or 3 in every 100 kids remain so afraid of separating that they cry continuously when away from their parents, or refuse to go to school altogether. This is often referred to as *school phobia.*

School phobia is a misnomer. Children aren't afraid of school; they are afraid of being separated from their parents (in which case we speak of them as suffering from *separation anxiety disorder*), or they are afraid of being around and interacting with other people (in which case we speak of them as suffering from, yes, *social anxiety disorder*). Either fear can result in the child wanting to avoid school. But the focus of treatment differs depending on the nature of the fear. It is therefore important to sort out the reason the child is resisting school.

We want to make one additional point here: no child should be allowed to choose not to go to school because of anxiety. If your child wants to stay home from school because he or she is too afraid to go, you should do two things. First, try to determine the cause of the fear. If it's legitimate (for instance, violence has occurred at school, the child is being bullied, or a teacher is being abusive), meet with the principal immediately. If the fear is irrational or excessive (your child has a problem with social anxiety or a related anxiety problem or phobia), arrange to meet with the school counselor.

Second, once you are certain your child is not in any real physical danger, send him or her back to school. Not a week later, not three days later, but the next day! We'll talk more about this in the next chapter. But it's such an important principle that we wanted to bring it up here.

Implications of Social Anxiety for Children and Adolescents

Recent national surveys find that approximately 5 percent of children and adolescents in the United States have social anxiety disorder. Because of their symptoms, most experience some type of impairment in school, at home, and in their relationships.

Young people with social anxiety may, over time, develop related problems. These include the following:

♦ *Loneliness.*   Socially anxious children tend to become isolated as they are unable to develop a normal network of friends. Often a socially anxious child will have one or two close friends and rely on them for all social interactions. But families relocate, kids change schools, and interests diverge, and it becomes necessary to establish new friendships. This is very difficult for socially anxious children, and it tends to become more difficult as they get older. Whereas parents can (and should) arrange play dates for their young children, this isn't appropriate for the middle school era and beyond. This is when socially anxious children often get left behind.

♦ *Low self-esteem.*   When we play and work with others and things go well, we feel good about ourselves, but these opportunities are limited for socially anxious children. Often, these children blame themselves for the things they can't do. They see other kids making friends and having fun and become angry at themselves for their inability to do so. When this goes on for a long time, low self-esteem can result.

♦ *Depression.*   Studies show that socially anxious adolescents risk developing major depression in later adolescence or early adulthood. Depression in children and adolescents is now recognized as a serious public health concern. And suicide is one of the leading causes of death among adolescents in developed countries. Loneliness and low self-esteem—both of which may be outcomes of untreated social anxiety—are risk factors for major depression and hence for suicide.

When to Worry

Is it safe to say that if neither parent nor teacher is aware of a child's social anxiety, there probably isn't a problem? Yes, most of the time that's a reasonable conclusion. Most children with social anxiety will exhibit some of the behaviors we have described. If these behaviors aren't apparent and your child seems to be developing normal friendships, it's unlikely you're overlooking serious difficulties.

Let's say, though, that you are concerned about the extent of your child's shyness. When should you worry? Answer these questions:

- ◆ Is my child avoiding social situations?
- ◆ Does my child spend too much time alone?
- ◆ Does my child express feelings of loneliness or boredom?
- ◆ Is the situation worsening or not improving?
- ◆ Are there others in the family who have (or had) problems with shyness or social anxiety?

If you answered *yes* to some of these questions, you should probably be thinking about ways to help your child overcome his or her shyness. Part Two of this book is devoted to self-help approaches for tackling social anxiety; Chap. 11 tells how to adjust them for children and adolescents. However, if your child is expressing thoughts of not wanting to live, or of thinking about doing something to hurt or kill himself or herself or others, seek professional help immediately.

Do Children Grow Out of It?

Many children are shy; most will overcome their shyness without special help. Even some severely anxious young children get better on their own. We believe that most children grow out of their shyness because they learn through repeated experiences that there is little need to be afraid to speak in front of others, that it is to their advantage to express themselves, and that it is no fun being quiet and alone. Through everyday interactions with peers, teachers, and other adults, their anxiety and fears dissipate.

But some children don't grow out of it. How do you know if your child is one of these? If there is a family history of anxiety or depression, the risk is increased. The longer children have problems with social anxiety, the less likely it is they will outgrow it. So if your child has had a problem since age 6 and now at age 10 isn't any better—or is worse—there's a greater chance the problem will persist. If your child is already showing signs of depression and low self-esteem, don't wait to see if he or she will outgrow it—intervene now.

The bottom line is that there is no surefire way of knowing whether your child will outgrow shyness. The best advice we can give is to encourage social behaviors in your child. Just as most parents want their children to learn to swim, most parents want to help their children become socially confident. The time you spend teaching your child these things is time well spent.

CHAPTER 5

Choosing the Right Treatment

O vercoming social phobia involves a significant commitment of time, effort, and, in some cases, money. To decide what approach is most suitable for you, you must have the right information. In this chapter we provide an overview of the kinds of treatments that are available through physicians, psychologists, and other mental health practitioners. We will also talk about self-help programs. In addition, we will discuss advantages and disadvantages of various treatments.

Good News and Bad News About Treatment

The good news is that there has been tremendous interest in the treatment of social anxiety in recent years. As a result, people have more treatment options today than ever before.

The bad news is that it may be hard to find someone experienced at treating social anxiety disorder in your community. Even when you find someone, he or she may recommend a course of therapy without providing much information about other treatments and their relative merits. Our goal is to provide information you can use to become a well-informed consumer and choose the treatment that best suits you.

Psychological Treatments for Shyness and Social Anxiety

Talk Therapies

These approaches involve a client and therapist working together. There is (or at least there should be) a solid theoretical basis for how the talk will lead to improvement in the condition(s) being addressed. The therapist's role is usually to facilitate change in the client's way of thinking, feeling, behaving, or approaching the problem. What goes on during therapy can vary markedly depending on the kind of therapy, and often on the style or personality of the therapist.

There are hundreds of different kinds of psychotherapy out there (more flavors than Baskin-Robbins). It would take a whole book—a very big book—to describe all the forms of psychotherapy practiced in the United States, Canada, Europe, and other industrialized nations. And probably another set of books to describe the range of psychotherapies practiced in other countries and cultures. We will focus on some mainstream treatments you may have heard of or read about. Not all treatments are equally effective, and you can't judge the effectiveness of a treatment merely by measuring the experience or credentials of the therapist providing it.

Cognitive-Behavioral Therapy. The form of psychological treatment that has the widest scientific support for addressing anxiety disorders is *cognitive-behavioral therapy (CBT)*. CBT focuses on understanding and changing thinking patterns (cognition) and behavior patterns that are involved in anxiety problems. When you change your thinking and behavior, emotional changes often follow. This approach to dealing with common problems including pain, anxiety and phobias, depression, relationship problems, and substance abuse has been evolving over the last 40 years. In CBT, approaches are developed to address specific problems; in fact, different forms of CBT have been developed for each anxiety disorder, including social anxiety. CBT for social anxiety requires the therapist to assess the client's problem, educate the client about the problem, and work with the client to develop strategies that will help overcome anxious thoughts, physical symptoms, and anxious behaviors.

CBT approaches have several aspects in common. They tend to be time-limited; that is, they try to accomplish the required changes in a limited number of sessions. This is an advantage of CBT, in that benefits are usually seen in weeks or months rather than years, and the costs are correspondingly lower than with treatments that require a longer time. Naturally, the actual time and cost involved will depend on the difficulty of the problem. For a flying phobia, the treatment might be three to six sessions, or one long session. For a more complicated problem such as generalized social anxiety disorder, 10 to 20 sessions are commonly planned.

CBT typically involves reading about the problem, keeping records about the problem between appointments, and doing homework assignments in which the treatment procedures are practiced. Practice is the heart and soul of CBT. Skills are learned during therapy sessions, but they are practiced—repeatedly—outside of the sessions. The more you practice, the more you improve. Because CBT teaches skills for handling anxiety, the person who does a good job learning and practicing these skills can call upon them when anxiety recurs. In other words, CBT may provide long-lasting benefits. This is a substantial advantage of CBT over medication.

You may participate in CBT through individual therapy, group therapy, or a self-help program (see Part Two).

Interpersonal Psychotherapy. *Interpersonal psychotherapy (IPT) is a form* of talk therapy that focuses on relationships. IPT is becoming increasingly popular for treating depression and related problems. The theory behind IPT is that depression is often rooted in relationship difficulties, and that people can be taught to improve the quality of these relationships. IPT has been proven effective in the treatment of mild to moderate clinical depression. Because people with shyness and social anxiety often have interpersonal difficulties, it has been suggested that IPT could be adapted to help

TIP: CONSIDER GROUP THERAPY.

Our socially anxious clients are often horrified when we suggest they attend a group program. But it turns out that a major advantage of group treatment is that it allows people to develop both confidence and coping strategies in a real-life social situation. Another advantage is the cost, which is usually substantially less than for individual therapy.

Consider a woman who is afraid of going in the water but wants to learn to swim. She could meet with a swimming instructor in her living room, watch videotapes, and discuss the actions involved in swimming. Or she could wade into the shallow end of the pool and work with the instructor in the water. Which method do you think is better? Working to overcome social anxiety in a group setting is like learning to swim in the water!

them. Some preliminary research has been promising, but we cannot yet say that IPT is effective against social anxiety.

Supportive Psychotherapy. A widely used form of therapy is *supportive psychotherapy* or *supportive counseling*. As the name suggests, the role of the therapist in this approach is to support the client in dealing with life stresses and solving problems. At times, the therapist assumes an active role, providing advice and making suggestions. There is not a lot of energy directed toward understanding the underlying or historical reasons for symptoms; instead, the therapist helps the client adopt practical approaches to solving current life problems. The therapist often also lends emotional support to help the client through times of crisis. Supportive psychotherapy is a flexible treatment, geared toward helping the client function despite ongoing difficulties. We are not aware of any studies showing that supportive psychotherapy can help overcome shyness or social anxiety. Our impression is that many people have found supportive psychotherapy helpful in dealing with life problems—some of which may be directly related to social anxiety and some of which may not.

Psychoanalysis and Analytically Oriented Psychotherapy. *Psychoanalysis* was one of the first forms of psychological treatment. Most of us have seen cartoons spoofing classical psychoanalysis, with the patient lying on a couch and the therapist sitting behind the couch, taking notes. In classical psychoanalysis, the analyst interprets the patient's dreams and verbalizations, guiding the patient toward an understanding of the origins of his or her anxiety. The theory behind this form of treatment usually stems from the writings of Sigmund Freud, Carl Jung, or their disciples. Few mental health providers nowadays practice classical psychoanalysis, but many still provide a form of *analytically oriented psychotherapy* that has at its core the same set of theoretical beliefs and principles.

There is not a lot of scientific evidence that analytically oriented psychotherapy is helpful in the treatment of shyness or social anxiety. This doesn't mean that it isn't helpful; it just means that it hasn't been evaluated for these kinds of problems. We have encountered many patients with social anxiety disorder who have spent long periods of time (often many years—and many dollars) in analytically oriented psychotherapy. We often hear them say that the treatment helped them better understand themselves, but they rarely say they found that the treatment helped lessen their social anxiety.

Virtual Reality Therapy

Virtual reality therapy (VRT) has generated a lot of interest recently for its use in the treatment of a range of phobia problems. For example, to treat a flying phobia, the client is hooked up to a virtual reality system that simulates the look and feel of an airplane in flight. Typically, the client is secured in a seat like that found on an airplane (depending on the system, the seat may vibrate to simulate turbulence). Goggles present a realistic picture of an aircraft environment, often with 360-degree capability. Headphones provide background sounds of the engines rumbling, the pilot issuing takeoff and landing warnings, thunder, and the like. Most clients say the simulation is very realistic. A course of VRT for flying phobia may involve anywhere from 6 to 10 sessions, guided by the therapist. VRT is not yet widely available, but this is likely to change in coming years. VRT has been so successful for treating flying phobias that new systems are being developed to simulate other anxiety-provoking situations, including public speaking. Whether it will prove beneficial for this and other forms of social anxiety remains to be determined.

Other Forms of Therapy

While *hypnosis* is sometimes used to treat anxiety and phobias, we are not aware of any studies that show it works for social anxiety.

Biofeedback is another form of therapy sometimes suggested for treatment of anxiety and phobias. Biofeedback involves the use of monitoring devices to give people information about their physiological functioning. Feedback may be provided about muscle tension, heart rate, skin perspiration, or brain waves. The person can then employ a technique such as relaxation to lower the level of arousal. There are some studies, most conducted many years ago, suggesting that biofeedback can be helpful in managing different kinds of anxiety and phobias. A disadvantage of the biofeedback approach is that it may require costly equipment that is not widely available. In most situations, it has not been shown to be more effective than relaxation training, which requires no more than a tape player or CD player. Therefore, we do not consider biofeedback an effective stand-alone treatment for social anxiety.

TIP: INVESTIGATE TREATMENT OPTIONS BEFORE MAKING A DECISION.

If you can find someone in your area who specializes in anxiety problems, feel free to ask questions about the services he or she provides. It is very acceptable, for example, to ask before your first meeting about the kind of treatment to be provided, the hourly cost, and the usual number of sessions. If a provider is not willing to answer reasonable questions about the service, including the cost, be cautious about dealing with that person.

Medication

Medication can help reduce social anxiety and severe shyness. Some drugs are useful only for performance anxiety (public speaking or playing a musical instrument in front of an audience) whereas others are more useful for treating generalized social anxiety (the kind that occurs in a broad array of social situations, often those involving interactions with others).

Some classes of medications that have been used to treat social anxiety are the following:

- *Beta blockers* such as Inderal or Tenormin
- *Benzodiazepines* such as Xanax or Klonopin
- *Selective serotonin reuptake inhibitor* (SSRI) *antidepressants* such as Paxil or Luvox

- *Other antidepressants* such as Effexor or Nardil
- *Herbal therapies* such as kava kava

An advantage of medications is that many physicians are familiar with using them to treat other conditions such as depression. They are also covered by many health insurance plans, whereas some psychological therapies may not be. This makes medication for social anxiety accessible for many persons who might otherwise not get any treatment. Disadvantages of medications include the possibility of side effects and the fact that medications work only as long as you continue taking them. We will review the use of medication for social anxiety in detail in Chap. 10.

Self-Help Treatments

Self-help treatments, which do not require the direct assistance of a physician or therapist, have grown in popularity as people seek ways to assume responsibility for their own wellness. Also, a self-help approach costs less than visiting a professional.

Self-help programs for shyness and social anxiety are often very successful, which is why we have written this book. Parts Two and Three provide a step-by-step program for breaking out of the social phobia cage.

TIP: IF YOU PANIC AT THE THOUGHT OF SPEAKING IN PUBLIC, DON'T TRY TO COPE IN PRIVATE—JOIN A GROUP.

There are several organizations in the business of helping people become more comfortable with public speaking. One of these, Toastmasters International, was established with the formation of the first Toastmasters Club in California in 1924. Today it has clubs in more than 60 countries. Many clubs have breakfast, lunch, or dinner meetings, with a modest charge in addition to an annual membership fee. Toastmasters was created to provide a supportive place where members could develop skills to conduct meetings and give both impromptu and prepared speeches. Prospective members typically attend one or two meetings as guests to see if they like it.

When you come to the first meeting, you are introduced to the other members but are not expected to do anything else. As you become familiar with the group, you are invited to participate more actively. For instance, after a few meetings, you might participate by giving a short introduction to a presentation by another club member. Toastmasters provides excellent information about how to give introductions and perform other typical public-speaking assignments. When you are ready, you start to work on your speaking skills, first with brief presentations, then gradually with longer ones. Speakers receive comments after each presentation, with an emphasis on positive criticism and suggestions for improvement. The opportunity for repeated practice in speaking situations, receiving constructive feedback and suggestions, and working at your own pace provides an ideal learning experience. For information about Toastmasters Clubs in your area, check your local telephone directory or visit their Web site at www.toastmasters.org.

International Training in Communication (ITC) International is similar to Toastmasters. It started as a program for women but now serves men, too. Check the local telephone directory or their Web site, www.itcintl.org. If neither of these organizations is available where you live, check your local educational facilities for courses in public speaking. Remember that facing the feared situation in gradual steps with repeated practice is essential to increasing your confidence. Many people who start out with intense anxiety about public speaking end up actually enjoying it.

Combining or Switching Treatments

One treatment doesn't fit all. While our self-help program can benefit virtually everyone with shyness and social anxiety, some persons may need additional treatment. If you are one of them, don't despair. Many people find they require medication to function optimally, while others need the help of a therapist.

Self-help books often give the impression that all people can do it alone, and if they can't, they just haven't tried hard enough. This simply isn't true. We have seen highly motivated persons use self-help programs and improve—but not enough. This happens. We don't know why. But it does happen. And when it does, we encourage the person to consider other therapies, typically medication or CBT.

What About Combining Treatments From the Start?

Since some people wind up needing a combination of treatments, would it be a good idea to just start that way? We don't usually recommend it. Most people do well enough with self-help alone, or with either medication or

CBT alone, and adding a second therapy at the beginning would be a waste of time and money.

We recommend a *sequential* approach instead. By this we mean that you start with one form of treatment, give it your best shot, and take stock of how much progress you have made before adding another treatment. For example, you might start by using the self-help program described in this book. You find that it has helped you, but there are still situations where your anxiety is out of control. You might then seek the help of a therapist to overcome these additional difficulties. After several sessions, you and your therapist may reach the conclusion that this hasn't been sufficiently helpful. You might then see a physician who can prescribe medication.

There is little information to help us predict who is likely to respond to a particular form of treatment, so mental health practitioners must hunt and peck for the best treatment for each client. We believe that it makes sense, though, to start with the least expensive and least cumbersome treatments—self-help, perhaps—follow up with therapy when necessary, and add medication when needed.

What About Starting with Medication?

No treatment is without side effects—even therapy can make people uncomfortable—and medications are no exception. In most cases, the side effects are minimal or at least quite tolerable (see Chap. 10). But the possibility of side effects is one reason you may prefer to try self-help or CBT before taking medication.

On the other hand, there are times when you should see a physician (either a family doctor who is comfortable with and experienced at handling mental health problems or a psychiatrist) and start on medication early in the course of treatment. Examples of such times would be if you are so depressed that you can't concentrate; you are having trouble separating reality from imagination (for instance, you are hearing voices), or you are having thoughts about hurting or killing yourself or anyone else. If you are experiencing these symptoms, you need the assistance of a professional. Self-help is not enough!

What if your family physician recommends that you take medication for social anxiety? By starting medication early in the course of treatment, some difficulties associated with social anxiety (depressed mood, for example) may improve. This may make it easier for you to embark on a self-help program, and is a valid reason to start on a medication sooner rather than later.

TIP: MAKE YOUR MEDICATION WORK FOR YOU.

Many physicians are still not familiar with the holistic treatment of social anxiety, though they may have some knowledge about the medications used to treat it. This may lead a doctor to prescribe a drug without telling you what you should do to maximize its effects, particularly in the long term. It is important to remember that medications will work while you take them, but once you stop taking them their effects gradually disappear. Medications do not *cure* social anxiety, although they can reduce it enough for you to practice being in situations that you were formerly too anxious to enter. Take this opportunity—while you are on the medication—to expose yourself to uncomfortable situations as much as possible (more about this in Part Two). The more you practice while you are taking the medication, the more your self-confidence will improve, and the more likely it is that your social anxiety will decrease.

Part Two

Helping Yourself Overcome Shyness and Social Anxiety

CHAPTER 6

Three Steps to Overcoming Social Anxiety

Y ou need to do three things to overcome your social anxiety:
1. Understand your anxiety pattern.
2. Change your thinking in anxiety-provoking situations.
3. Change your anxious behaviors.

If you make a commitment to follow these three steps, you will dramatically reduce your social anxiety. For any kind of program to be successful—whether it's self-help, individual therapy, or group therapy—you must make it a priority. The first step is to read through the program quickly (you don't have to do the exercises the first time through) and decide if you are willing to commit to it. If you are, the next step is to follow through and spend time on the program every day for two or three months. This is a significant commitment and may require that you cut down on other activities, at least temporarily.

Who Benefits from Self-Help Programs?

We were skeptical at first about the ability of self-help books to deal with anxiety. This changed as people told us of their experiences in using such books. We frequently met people who had suffered with a serious anxiety problem for years and not understood it until they read a book or a magazine article and were then able to find help. We remember a woman who came for help in dealing with fears and phobias. As we discussed the history of the problem, she mentioned that it had been much worse before she read a book by Dr. Susan Jeffers, *Feel the Fear and Do It Anyway*. This book gave her information that enabled her to overcome the problem. She came to our program looking for additional help years later.

Because of these experiences, we have been recommending high-quality educational and self-help materials for many years. One experience stands out:

Jim had volunteered for a study evaluating a program to help people with social anxiety. Jim's social anxiety limited his performance in business situations and his social life. He was very anxious about speaking at business meetings. Inviting someone for a date was so anxiety provoking that he rarely dated.

Jim was busy, and it was difficult to arrange a convenient time to meet. Finally, we met; we gave him the book and workbook used in the program and told him the date and location of the first session. Later, we found that Jim had not made it to a single meeting. When we met with him four months later as part of the evaluation of the program, we expected him to tell us he had been too busy to work on the problem. We were flabbergasted by his story.

He had read the book the day we gave it to him. He had started to apply the program's principles in everyday life and could see the progress he was making. Before long he worked up the courage to join a course in standup comedy at a local comedy club. Several months later, he participated in the graduating exercise—10 minutes on stage during open-mike night! You could feel his excitement about his progress. Business meetings were now much easier, and he planned to start dating.

Now, many of us would be horrified at the prospect of performing at a comedy club (ourselves included), but we were struck by how much progress Jim made on his own. We find that people who commit to working on the program every day and practice the procedures in their everyday lives benefit most from self-help programs. If you feel that you cannot make this commitment, or if you work hard at the program for a couple of months and make only limited progress, the knowledge you gain will help you resolve the problem in the future. In either case, we encourage you to seek professional help (see Chap. 4).

Understanding Your Pattern of Social Anxiety

Anxiety is a normal human emotion, the emotion that motivates humans (and animals, for that matter) to keep themselves safe. One aspect of the protective anxiety system is the *fight or flight response.* When you encounter danger, the body automatically prepares for self-preservation: you prepare yourself to either defend against an attacker (*fight*) or to flee (*flight*). A related part of this protective system is to *freeze* in a dangerous situation so as not to attract attention. You may have seen a rabbit or a deer freeze when it becomes aware that there are humans—potential predators—around. In stressful social situations some people find themselves freezing, unable to say or do anything.

While the anxiety response involves many bodily systems acting in a coordinated fashion, it is helpful to consider separate aspects of the response. In the pages that follow we will consider three systems involved in the anxiety response: anxious physical reactions, anxious thoughts, and anxious behaviors.

Anxious Physical Reactions

You often first become aware of anxiety by noticing your physical reactions. You may notice your heart racing or your face flushing. The level of activity in your stomach and the rest of your gastrointestinal (GI) system may increase, creating discomfort in your stomach or a feeling that you need to have a bowel movement. You may perspire excessively. As your level of bodily arousal increases, you become especially watchful for signs of danger or threat. You may feel that your body is betraying you and making it more difficult to cope with anxiety. People who experience social anxiety may be especially concerned about symptoms that others may notice: blushing, excessive perspiration, shaky hands, or a noisy stomach. Here are some examples:

Michelle: "I can't stand this growling stomach."

Michelle, a dancer, became aware that her stomach was sometimes noisy in social situations. This embarrassed her, and she started to avoid recitals and parties. If she had an audition, she would hold her dance bag over her stomach and sit away from other people, close to the door. Dating was difficult, as were gatherings with friends. She struggled with this problem even though her stomach did not growl that often.

Nancy: "I wish I wouldn't blush."

Nancy had blond hair and a fair complexion, and was troubled over the years by her tendency to blush when having a conversation. She tried to cope by avoiding social situations. She preferred not to have lunch or take coffee breaks with coworkers. She considered applying for a promotion but decided against it because she might have to attend more meetings.

Steve: "The sweating is so embarrassing."

Steve lived with his parents and had few friends. He found social situations difficult because whenever he had to mingle with other people, perspiration dripped steadily from his armpits. Whenever possible, he would wear a sweatshirt to hide the wet spots under his arms. This condition limited his career choices, because he couldn't take a job where he had to wear a business shirt.

For Michelle, Nancy, and Steve, the physical reaction to anxiety is the most disturbing part of the response. (We'll say more in Chap. 8 about strategies to cope with bodily symptoms.) For others, the psychological component of anxiety is the worst.

Imagine that it's Friday at 5:15. You get a voicemail message that there was an error in one of your assignments, a project completed two months ago and scheduled to be discussed at a meeting on Monday morning. There is no chance to find out what the problem is before the meeting, and you are left to stew about it over the weekend.

What thoughts do you have? It is likely that you think about past assignments and try to remember which ones may have had problems. You wonder what questions they will ask you at the meeting and whether you will be able to answer them. You worry about how this problem will affect your future at the company. As you think about these things, anxiety surges through your body. You feel overheated, your heart races, and you are sick to your stomach. Throughout the weekend, you are unable to concentrate when you try to read or watch television. You toss and turn as thoughts about the problem plague you even when you try to sleep.

In addition to the uncomfortable physical symptoms, a major aspect of anxiety is what you *think* about a situation. When you perceive a social situation as difficult, threatening, or anxiety provoking, this assessment will color not only your experience during the interaction, but your perceptions of it *before* and *after* the event, as well.

Before a Situation. Your thinking may be marked by anticipatory anxiety—anxiety before the situation actually occurs—about what will happen and doubts about whether you will be able to handle it. You may visualize the situation turning out badly and imagine you will feel embarrassed or humiliated. These worries are often *intrusive;* that is, they come to you when you are trying to think about something else. Here are some examples of anxious thoughts before a challenging social encounter:

♦ What if I blush (sweat, shake) during the meeting?

♦ What if people see how nervous I am? What will they think of me?

♦ What if my mind goes blank and I'm not able to answer questions?

- What if people think I'm stupid when they hear what I say?
- What if people think I'm not as competent as everyone else?

During a Situation. The anxiety may peak as the interaction starts, or it may build gradually. Concentration may be difficult; rather than listen to what other people are saying, you may focus on your anxious thoughts and physical reactions. Here are some examples of anxious thoughts during a situation:

- When is the meeting going to start? I hope it's over soon.
- That person looks angry. Is he angry with me?
- What do people think of what I'm saying?
- Will someone say things that upset me?

After a Situation. You are usually relieved to be finished, and the level of physical symptoms often decreases. After the initial relief, though, thoughts turn to how you handled the encounter. When you are having difficulty with anxiety, your evaluation of your performance is often negative. Here are some examples of negative thoughts after a situation:

- They must have seen how nervous I was.
- What did people think of me? I bet they thought I was a real idiot.
- I made a fool of myself.
- They think I'm incompetent.
- They won't want to be involved with me in the future.

These negative thoughts before, during, and after social situations feed the anxiety. We will be saying more in later chapters about how you can change the negative thinking that feeds anxiety.

Anxious Behaviors: Coping Strategies
That May Do More Harm Than Good

Certain behaviors are emblematic of social anxiety, two of the most common being *avoidance behavior* and *escape behavior*.

Avoidance behavior manifests itself when you try to stay away from situations that make you anxious. Avoidance behavior is a useful strategy when it keeps you out of dangerous situations, like taking a midnight stroll through Central Park with dollar bills taped to your body. But when your perception of which situations are dangerous and should be avoided includes social gatherings, educational sessions, and business meetings, this is no longer an adaptive strategy. It is at this point that avoidance dominates your life. Avoidance also prevents you from learning ways to challenge social anxiety and overcome the problem.

Another common anxiety symptom is *escape behavior.* Escape behavior involves leaving an anxiety-arousing situation. If you have trouble conversing with certain types of people, you might escape by having a few words and then giving an excuse about needing to leave to finish something. If parties make you anxious, you might escape by pretending to have a family emergency and leaving the party 10 minutes after you arrive.

There is a range of behaviors people use to cope with social anxiety. Are any of these familiar to you?

+ Staying close to a trusted friend (or your spouse) at a gathering and relying on that person to do most of the talking
+ Remaining in one location at a gathering; trying to converse with one or two people and not mingle with the others
+ Staying in the kitchen at a party and helping with the food preparation or cleanup
+ Having a few glasses of wine before going to a dinner party and a few more when you arrive
+ Going to the bathroom frequently to get away from people
+ Spending hours rehearsing a two-minute wedding toast

Most of us will recognize some of these behaviors as ones we have used at some point in our lives. We didn't have much trouble coming up with the list because we have used all these strategies ourselves.

Putting It All Together: Physical Reactions, Thoughts, and Behaviors

We can talk about the three systems involved in anxiety—physical reactions, thoughts, and behaviors—separately, but, in fact, they all work together. Each system is influenced by the others. Our thoughts about challenging situations influence our physical reactions. Our physical reactions influence our thoughts. Similarly, our behavior is influenced by both, and in turn influences both. This is illustrated in Fig. 6.1.

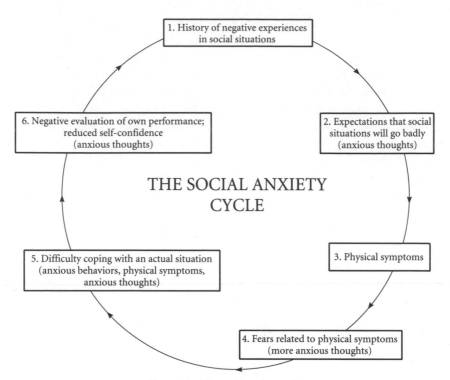

Figure 6.1   The social anxiety cycle.

Describing Your Own Experience of Social Anxiety

Completing the worksheets in Figs. 6.2 to 6.4 will help you become aware of your own anxiety symptoms. You will use this information later to develop coping strategies. We encourage you to go ahead and mark your answers in the book—don't just answer in your head. Marking the answers makes it easier for you to come back and check your responses for the work you will be doing later on. If you think you might want to lend the book to someone later, use pencil, or photocopy the pages. Better yet, we will gladly sell you more books for your friends!

Social Anxiety Symptoms

In difficult social situations, how much are you distressed by the following physical symptoms? Place a check mark in the appropriate box.

	Not at all	A little bit	Moderately	Quite a bit	Extremely
Blushing					
Feeling flushed (too hot)					
Feeling too cold					
Sweating					
Shaking or trembling					
Rapid heart rate					
Chest pain or discomfort					
Upset stomach, nausea					
Dry mouth					
Feeling of having to go to the toilet					
Faintness					
Dizziness or unsteadiness					
Numbness or tingling					
Difficulty breathing					
Difficulty swallowing; a choking feeling					
Feelings of unreality					
Feeling physically immobilized					
Mind going blank					
Difficulty concentrating					
Tense or twitching muscles					
Other:					

Figure 6.2 Social anxiety symptoms worksheet.

Anxious Thoughts

In difficult social situations, how much are you distressed by the following anxious thoughts?

	Not at all	A little bit	Moderately	Quite a bit	Extremely
I won't know what to say.					
My mind will go blank.					
I'll stumble over my words.					
I will make a mistake when I speak.					
I will be physically awkward.					
I will do something to embarrass myself.					
People will see that I'm nervous.					
People will watch me or stare at me					
People will have a negative impression of me.					
My nervousness will make people uncomfortable.					

Figure 6.3 Anxious thoughts worksheet.

	Not at all	A little bit	Moderately	Quite a bit	Extremely
People won't want to be around me.					
People won't like the way I look.					
People will think I'm foolish.					
People will think I'm too quiet.					
People will think I'm boring.					
People will laugh at me.					
People won't like me.					
Other:					
Other:					
Other:					
Other:					
Other:					

Figure 6.3 *Continued.*

Situations I Avoid

How much do you avoid the following social situations?

	Never	Seldom	Sometimes	Often	Always
Making eye contact with someone I don't know well					
Speaking before a large group of people					
Speaking before a small group of people					
Being the center of attention					
Attending social gatherings in general					
Going to a party					
Eating in public					
Speaking to people in authority (supervisor, teacher)					
Speaking with someone I'm attracted to					
Returning items to a store					
Writing in front of other people					
Having someone watch me while I do something					
Asking a question in a class or at a meeting					
Inviting a family member to visit my home					
Inviting a non–family member to visit my home					

Figure 6.4   Social avoidance worksheet.

	Never	Seldom	Sometimes	Often	Always
Calling someone I know well on the phone					
Calling someone I don't know well on the phone					
Asking someone for information					
Disagreeing with someone					
Other:					
Other:					

Figure 6.4 *Continued.*

Establishing Your Goals

As you plan to overcome your anxiety, it's important to start by considering your goals. Many people find it hard to think about what they want out of life because they can't imagine living without the limits imposed by anxiety. They can't see the honey for the bees (or something like that). Here are some examples of how anxiety may interfere with your goals:

- ◆ You would like to say something in a meeting or at coffee break, but are too shy to make a comment.
- ◆ You would like to take a night school course, but can't imagine being comfortable in a classroom.
- ◆ You would like to get a better job, but can't imagine handling the demands of a new position.
- ◆ You would like to have more friends or a romantic relationship (or both), but can't imagine how you would go about it.
- ◆ You would like to take a vacation, but can't imagine traveling on an airplane because of your fear of flying. (Oops, this one was taken from the fear of flying list. We'll have more to say later about making mistakes.)

Setting goals will keep you motivated to overcome anxiety. In approaching this task, it is important to put your fears aside and imagine a life unhampered by fear. You can worry later about how you will reach your goals and dreams, but for now, focus on deciding what they are.

Later in this chapter you will find two goal sheets—a completed sample and a blank one. Read through the instructions carefully, and spend some time imagining how your life would be if you could accomplish your goals. The goals are divided into three time frames: *long-term goals* (goals which may take more than a year or two to accomplish), *medium-term goals* (which can be accomplished in about one year), and *short-term goals* (which can be accomplished over a few months).

As you choose goals in each area, be as *specific* and *concrete* as possible. We have listed strong examples and weak examples to guide you. Include some goals that involve overcoming anxiety in challenging social situations. Do not restrict yourself, however, to these goals, as this would give an unbalanced view of what you hope to achieve. Make a few copies of the goal sheet to allow yourself to brainstorm first, and then fine-tune your list as you continue to work on it.

TRAP: **Avoid just thinking about your goals.**

- Avoid the temptation to make this strictly a mental exercise without putting your words on paper. Completing the goal sheet and putting your ideas on paper will help you commit to working steadily to overcome problems.
- One thought many people have when they start thinking about setting goals is, "What if I set a goal I can't reach? Will I feel like a failure?"

   Remember that this is a brainstorming exercise. All of us in the course of our lives will consider goals we will not reach. If life is going well, we set some goals aside to work on other ones. It is also normal to change goals as we move through life. Goals help guide our thoughts and actions even if they do change over time. If you haven't thought about where you are going in life, don't be surprised if you don't get there.

Long-Term Goals

Start by thinking about your long-term goals. What would you want from your life if you weren't socially anxious? What job would you want? Where would you like to live? Would you go further in school? Where would you go on vacation? What new hobbies would you start? Would you make new friends? Would you date more or solidify a current relationship? Let your imagination go free.

Make your list specific and concrete. We would all like to be happy and live with minimal anxiety, but these goals are too general. You need specific goals to guide you toward your more general goals. There is space for you to list five long-term goals, but feel free to write down as many as you can think of. Get a blank sheet of paper and have fun imagining a new life!

Strong Example. *"Take a winter vacation in the Bahamas every two years."* This is a strong example because it is specific and concrete—you can tell exactly what you want to do, and you'll know when you have done it.

Weak Example. *"Be happy and never feel anxiety again."* This is a weak example for two reasons. First, it is not specific and concrete—how can you tell when you've actually achieved it? What do you have to do to be happy? Second, anxiety is a normal, healthy part of life that everyone experiences at one time or another. It is not reasonable to expect to live completely free of anxiety. On the other hand, it is realistic to live a life in which anxiety is a minor factor.

Medium-Term Goals

These are goals you can imagine accomplishing *in the next year*. They may be steps on the way to your long-term goals. They may be activities you have avoided because of excessive shyness or anxiety. Once again, be very specific and concrete.

Strong Example. *"Start a course in medical terminology at Wilson College in the spring."* This is a strong example because it is specific and concrete—it states what you want to study and where you plan to study it—and may move you toward your long-term goal of an interesting career. The wording of the goal describes what you will have to do to attain it and makes it easy to tell when you have achieved it.

Weak Example. *"Go back to school."* This is a weak example because it is not specific enough. What school do you mean? What course do you want to take? When are you planning to do it? We often don't get around to working on vague goals.

Short-Term Goals

These are goals you can work on *in the next three months*. You may want to take one of your medium-term goals and break it down so you can start to work on parts of it right away. Think of at least eight short-term goals you can start working toward in the next three months. Be sure to set goals that will move you closer to your medium-term goals. Make your short-term goals specific and practical.

Strong Examples

"Take a tai-chi class at the community center next month."

"Eat lunch at Bistro Gardens with Steve."

"Ask a question at the staff meeting at work."

These are strong examples because they are manageable enough to work on soon and specific enough so you know what you should be doing and when you have done it.

Weak Examples

"Get some exercise."

"Go to a restaurant."

"Speak up more and not feel nervous."

These are weak examples. None of them is specific enough. What sort of exercise do you want to do? Where will you do it? What restaurant do you want to go to? Do you want to go alone or with someone? In what setting do you want to speak? Again, the goal of not feeling nervous is unrealistic. If you insist that your success be defined by doing things without any anxiety, you will probably feel you have failed. Doing things *in spite of anxiety* and managing the feelings are more reasonable goals. As you meet these goals, anxiety will decrease with continued practice.

Before filling out your goal sheet, look over the sample in Fig. 6.5. Note that the goals are specific and concrete. Also, go back to the worksheet in Fig. 6.4 and review the situations you avoid. Consider remaining in these situations as potential goals and write some on your goal sheet (Fig. 6.6).

Now, fill out your own goal sheet. Keep your goal sheet when it is done, because you will be reviewing your goals repeatedly as you work on the program.

TIP: SET AMBITIOUS GOALS.

Remember to set goals as if shyness and anxiety did not interfere with your activities. Don't let your anxiety prevent you from listing goals that are important to you.

GOAL SHEET   DATE: *April 6, 2002*

As you complete this sheet, think about not only your goals for overcoming anxiety problems but also your goals for the rest of your life—your career and home life, for example.

After you have listed your goals, rank them according to difficulty, with one being most difficult.

Long-Term Goals	Rank from 1 to 5
1. *Finish bachelor's degree*	*2*
2. *Visit Maria in Florida*	*5*
3. *Move to the country*	*3*
4. *Review career path and start upgrading skills*	*1*
5. *Learn to ski*	*4*

Medium-Term Goals (One Year):	Rank from 1 to 5
1. *Take a university course in spring*	*1*
2. *One-week vacation to Vancouver—summer*	*4*
3. *Take public speaking course*	*2*
4. *Join aerobics class at YMCA*	*3*
5. *Go to baseball games regularly with friends*	*5*

Short-Term Goals (Three Months):	Rank from 1 to 8
1. *Go for coffee break with Mike and Ellie*	*8*
2. *Ask questions in the staff meeting at work*	*2*
3. *Go to family dinners at least once a month*	*4*
4. *Have dinner at the Roasted Cow with one friend*	*6*
5. *Go to party with friends and stay until 1 A.M.*	*1*
6. *Make eye contact with supervisor when talking to her*	*3*
7. *Have Judy and Richard over for dinner*	*5*
8. *Call Allison and ask her to meet me for coffee*	*7*

Figure 6.5 Sample goal sheet.

GOAL SHEET   DATE:_____

As you complete this sheet, think about not only your goals for overcoming anxiety problems but also your goals for the rest of your life—your
career and home life, for example.

   After you have listed your goals, rank them according to difficulty, with
one being most difficult.

Long-Term Goals   Rank from 1 to 5
   1. _____
   2. _____
   3. _____
   4. _____
   5. _____

Medium-Term Goals (One Year):   Rank from 1 to 5
   1. _____
   2. _____
   3. _____
   4. _____
   5. _____

Short-Term Goals (Three Months):   Rank from 1 to 8
   1. _____
   2. _____
   3. _____
   4. _____
   5. _____
   6. _____
   7. _____
   8. _____

Figure 6.6   Goal sheet.

CHAPTER 7

Conquering Anxious Thoughts

Negative thinking is at the heart of social anxiety. Learning to change negative thinking patterns takes consistent practice, but this work can pay off with a dramatic decrease in anxiety. In this chapter we will discuss two aspects of anxious thinking—the focus of your thoughts, and the content of your thoughts.

The Focus of Your Thoughts

Excessive Self-Consciousness: Paul

Paul, age 30, was accepted to medical school after working for several years as a computer programmer. Going to medical school had been a lifelong goal. He had experienced difficulty with social anxiety throughout his life, and the many small group discussions required of medical students felt like torture.

Paul struggled with intense self-consciousness. He arrived early at class to take a seat near the door and away from the instructor, preferably at one of the corners of the large table. While in class, he worried constantly. Did he move around in his chair too much because he was so nervous? How should he place his hands and his arms? How did his facial expression and smile appear to others? What about the tone of his voice? When he asked a question, how did others react? Did people think he talked too much? Not enough? Would the students and instructors see how nervous he was? Some of the other students seemed uncomfortable also. Was this because he made them nervous? He was older than most of the others; would this create a negative impression? He began to think that he would have to drop out of the program and abandon his dream.

People with high levels of self-consciousness spend a great deal of time focusing on themselves rather than on the world around them. They focus on their feelings, thoughts, and actions, and on trying to guess how others are reacting to them.

Excessive self-focus causes several problems:

♦ It increases your anxiety level. Having someone watch and criticize your performance is distracting and stressful, even if that someone is you.

♦ It takes your attention away from other people, so you might miss important information.

♦ If you are distracted, others may assume you aren't interested in them, and respond to you less warmly.

Focusing More on Others and Less on Yourself

An important way to reduce social anxiety is to learn to shift your attention from yourself to other people. We all have some degree of control over our attention, and can choose to focus on some aspect of the situations we are in.

Think of listening to music. You can focus and listen especially carefully to the drums, the horns, or the piano. You may have to keep reminding yourself to focus on the piano. Other aspects of the music may capture your attention for awhile (listening to the drums when they are prominent) but you are able to keep your attention coming back to the piano. If you practice regularly, you become more skillful at focusing, and you can describe things about the piano parts that you did not hear before.

Your attention works the same way when you interact with people. If you practice focusing your attention on the other person rather than yourself, you will learn to be more attentive. Over time, this will help you cope more effectively with social situations while experiencing a lower level of anxiety. Here is a process you can follow:

♦ When you are feeling anxious, remind yourself to focus on others.

♦ Make it your goal to listen carefully to what the other person has to say.

♦ Think about how that person feels about what he or she is saying. Is this a situation involving strong emotion? Is this important information for that person? Or is he or she just passing on routine information?

♦ Often your attention will move back to yourself—especially when you are having an anxious thought or physical sensation. Don't worry about trying to stop these feelings from coming. Just accept them, and direct your attention back to the other person.

♦ Don't spend much time planning or rehearsing what you will say next. This will distract you from listening to the other person's side of the conversation. If you listen carefully, your own ideas about what to say next usually come quickly. (We will be saying more in later chapters about what to say in challenging situations.)

♦ Don't try to figure out what others are thinking about you during the situation. (This is called *mind reading*—something most of us can't do!)

Use this approach in one-on-one interactions, with groups of people, and at meetings. Focusing your attention on others can be difficult at first. Keep at it, because you will improve with practice.

TIP: SHOW YOUR INTEREST IN OTHERS.

Good conversational strategies will create a better impression on others than worrying about what they think of you. Remembering names, making eye contact, nodding when others are speaking, really listening to what they say, asking about their point of view, and finding out what they are interested in all pay off tremendously. If you don't have time for a conversation, just a couple of friendly words, spoken with a smile—"Hi, how are you today?"—will do.

Feeling Like the Center of Attention

Many people have trouble with excessive self-consciousness when they feel they are the center of attention. Here are some examples.

Marla: "Everyone is looking at me!"

Marla was extremely uncomfortable when she rode the bus. Getting on and walking down the aisle with everyone facing her was especially difficult. She did not know where to look and was reluctant to make eye contact with the other passengers. When she was seated, she felt that people were watching her, and she worried that she might do something embarrassing, like drop her parcels. She also worried that other people would find her or her clothing unattractive. She was so tense that she would walk two or three miles rather than take the bus.

A basis of excessive self-consciousness is the belief that other people are tremendously interested in your every action and are waiting to criticize you. The reality of life is very different. Each of us is the center of his or her own universe. We spend a great deal of time planning our actions and responding to other events in our lives. You may make the erroneous assumption that other people are just as interested in you as you are. In reality, other people use most of their time and attention dealing with their *own* lives. They have a small amount of time to pay attention to you. If they happen to see that you are nervous or uncomfortable, they may think about this for a short time, and then they have to get on with their personal concerns. They are unlikely to go through the day remembering an incident that has happened to you, even if you do. Most reasonable people are not terribly critical of others. If a person is very critical, he or she may not be the kind of person you want to have a relationship with anyway.

When people are in public situations (such as riding a bus or sitting in a shopping mall) it is common to pass the time by *people watching*. Young men watch for attractive young women and vice versa. People look at what clothing others are wearing, how they arrange their hair and jewelry, what they are carrying, where they might be going, and so on. Most people's memories of what they see are short-lived. There are ways of getting extra attention, such as by having a small child, a pet, or an unusual piece of clothing or hairdo, but most of us hold other people's attention for only a brief time. Cultures have unwritten rules about people watching. It is okay to look at someone when he or she is not looking at you, but it is considered rude to stare at someone when he or she is looking your way. If someone *does* look your way when you are looking, and you feel comfortable with that person, it is considered reasonable to smile briefly.

Marla recalled that although she tried to avoid eye contact, she also passed the time by watching other people. When she said to herself while riding the bus, "People watching is normal," she found she was able to relax more. (This is an example of a *coping thought,* something we'll come back to later in this chapter.) Soon Marla was able to enjoy doing what other people do when they are on the bus—watching people!

Antennae Out for Signs of Disapproval: Phil

Phil was a management consultant assigned to work in the headquarters of a large client, which had cubicles rather than offices. Phil was very self-conscious and disliked talking on the telephone when someone might overhear. He had regular telephone contacts with his supervisor, who routinely asked about problems with the assignment. Phil became worried that he might be violating the client's confidentiality by discussing these problems with his supervisor. One day, Phil noticed that a coworker who often disagreed with him about technical issues seemed to be treating him coolly. It suddenly hit him that she might have overheard his conversation and complained to management.

That afternoon, the client's senior manager told Phil he wanted to meet with him the next day. Phil was overwhelmed with worry and pictured himself clearing off his desk and being escorted from the office by a security officer. He slept little that night and could hardly eat his breakfast the next morning. When he finally met with the manager, he told him that the firm was very pleased with his work and wanted him to take on a new project.

Phil's situation is an example of the problem with being on the lookout for rejection. When your antennae are feeling for negative reactions, you can easily misinterpret cues (in this case, a coworker's coolness).

We frequently see both sides of a situation in group therapy sessions. One night, a woman named Barbara wept while discussing a difficult problem. She later said that she felt terribly embarrassed about losing control and making a fool of herself in front of the group. At the next session, when we asked group members about their reactions, they said they understood Barbara's feelings, and that she helped them understand their own feelings. This helped Barbara—and the other group members—realize that most people are pretty understanding, and that showing strong emotion at times is completely acceptable.

TIP: FOCUS ON THE TASK AT HAND, *NOT* THOSE WHO MAY BE WATCHING YOU.

Many people find it especially difficult to have other people watch them while they are working. At times this is an incidental part of an activity— such as when a graphic arts instructor observes a student, when a student watches a teacher, or when a manager accompanies a sales rep on a call. Even more challenging is a situation where being observed is part of the evaluation process, such as when you take a road test for your driver's license. In these situations, it is important to keep your focus on the activity and not on the person observing you. It is also helpful to keep in mind the purpose of the activity—to help you learn, to demonstrate your learning, or to enable the observer to give you (usually helpful) feedback on the quality of your performance.

We all receive some criticism as part of the learning process. You need to learn to handle this calmly, without taking it personally. If you find that you are facing a lot of criticism in your life, it may be coming from only one person or a small group of people (a family member or supervisor at work, for example). It is more effective to focus on dealing with a problem with a person than to be overly vigilant about negative reactions or criticism from others. Coping thoughts (described later in this chapter) and practicing remaining in challenging situations (outlined in Chap. 9 on changing your anxious behaviors) can also help you deal with these situations.

Refocusing Attention Worksheet

The idea of learning to change your focus of attention is new to most people. When you read the previous sections, did you feel that some of the descriptions fit your situation? The best way to see if excessive self-consciousness or concern about criticism and rejection are problems for you is to think about challenging situations you have faced in the past. Complete the worksheet in Fig. 7.1 to describe situations where this may have been a problem.

Refocusing Attention Worksheet

1. Challenging situation:

_____

_____

Any problems with excessive self-consciousness or concern about criticism or rejection? ,

_____

If yes, what could you focus on instead?

_____

_____

2. Challenging situation:

_____

_____

Any problems with excessive self-consciousness or concern about criticism or rejection?

_____

If yes, what could you focus on instead?

_____

_____

3. Challenging situation:

_____

_____

Any problems with excessive self-consciousness or concern about criticism or rejection?

_____

If yes, what could you focus on instead?

_____

_____

4. Challenging situation:

_____

_____

Any problems with excessive self-consciousness or concern about criticism or rejection?

_____

If yes, what could you focus on instead?

_____

_____

Figure 7.1   Refocusing attention worksheet.

Dealing with Anticipatory Anxiety

The strategy of focusing your attention on the other people in a social situation can be very effective for handling the situation itself. However, you may find yourself struggling with a great deal of anxiety in anticipation of a challenging encounter. For example, you may worry for weeks in advance about the annual company holiday party. In many cases this *anticipatory anxiety* lasts much longer and creates more stress than the situation itself.

Ask yourself: "How much time have I spent worrying about the situation?" and then, "How much time have I spent planning for the situation?" Typically, people answer that they have spent many hours worrying and little or no time planning. Shifting this balance from worrying (which accomplishes nothing other than making you more anxious) to planning (doing things in advance of the situation that may help it go more smoothly) can make the difference between feeling overwhelmed and feeling well prepared.

TIP: SOLVE PROBLEMS WITH PEN AND PAPER.

Use a pen and paper to briefly describe:

- The problem situation
- What you would like to accomplish
- Several alternative ways of handling the situation
- The advantages and disadvantages of each alternative

Choose the alternative that makes the most sense to you based on experience. You may even want to develop a short script about the important points you want to bring up in an interaction. Planning in advance will free you to focus more on the other person when you are in the interaction. Avoid the temptation to do your planning without pen and paper. Mental planning often just becomes part of the worry cycle.

TRAP: Avoid overplanning.

Although problem solving is very useful, some people spend too much time in the planning phase. An example would be spending eight hours working on a 20-minute presentation. Be sure to think through how much planning time is necessary; good planning is often done in a short period of time. Do not spend many hours planning for every possible catastrophe. This is just another type of worry.

Dealing with a Stressful Phone Call: Sara

Sara received a phone message at work. She planned to return the call promptly but was too nervous and let it fall to the bottom of her to do list. The following week, she received another message from the person asking her to call back. It was too late that day to return the call, but Sara worried that returning the call the next day would be even worse. Would the caller be irate about her not calling back more promptly? Would the caller present her with a difficult problem?

Rather than just worry about the situation, Sara decided to take a problem-solving approach. Here are the notes she made for herself:

What is the problem?

I don't like making phone calls and I have been too slow in getting back to this person.

I'm not sure what she wants to talk about and I am worried that it is something I won't be able to handle.

Now that I have waited so long before calling back, I am feeling guilty and worried about whether she will be angry with me.

Possible solutions:

I could ignore the call and hope that she gives up or decides to call someone else. If I do this, she might complain. I also won't learn anything about handling difficult situations.

I could schedule a time to call her tomorrow before I get too involved in other work. I could apologize for my delay in calling her back. If she asks me something difficult I can make some notes and promise to get back to her later that day.

Phone script:

Hello. This is Sara Jimenez calling from RSVPizza. I received your message yesterday and realized that I hadn't returned your earlier call. I would like to apologize for the delay in getting back to you. We have been very busy and I have had trouble returning all my calls. [Wait for reply] How may I help you? [If difficult problem] I'll need to check into that. Is there a convenient time when I could call you back after I do some checking?

Sara felt better just knowing that she had a plan to deal with the call. She would take care of this as soon as possible on the next business day. She put the planning notes and script in her purse so they would be handy as soon as she arrived at work.

When your anticipatory anxiety persists in spite of good planning, other strategies can be helpful, particularly facing your fear. (See Chap. 9.)

Healthy and Unhealthy Distraction

When you are anxious, distracting yourself (thinking about something else) can help manage the anxiety. But distraction can be healthy or unhealthy, depending on how you use it.

Here are some examples:

- Your heart is pounding and butterflies are fluttering in your stomach while you are in a meeting at work.

    Healthy distraction: Rather than pay attention to the symptoms, you pay attention to what the other people are saying and take notes to help you follow up.

    Unhealthy distraction: You start to daydream about the coming weekend and what you will be doing to relax. You miss a lot of the information discussed at the meeting.

- You have studied all day for tomorrow's exam and are well prepared but still worried about how the exam will go.

    Healthy distraction: You plan to take a break and see a movie rather than tire yourself out with more studying.

    Unhealthy distraction: You study until 2 A.M., awake exhausted, and are less able to concentrate.

- You have been worrying about an upcoming meeting with your supervisor and feel nauseated.

    Healthy distraction: You get out a piece of paper and spend 15 minutes making notes covering the issues you'd like to discuss. You then move on to the rest of your work for the day.

    Unhealthy distraction: You arrange to meet some friends at a bar. One drink becomes five, and you come to work the next day unprepared for the meeting and with a hangover to boot.

- You are on deadline for an assignment and don't think you can get the work done in time.

Healthy distraction: You have an hour before you leave for a meeting so you decide to review one of the background papers for the assignment.

Unhealthy distraction: You take a long coffee break before the meeting and put off the assignment until tomorrow.

Healthy distraction often involves focusing on an activity that will be helpful to you in the long run. Unhealthy distraction may involve activities such as working excessively, using alcohol, watching television, or sleeping.

The Content of Your Thoughts
Thoughts, Beliefs, and Assumptions

Scientists who spend their time thinking about thinking (nice work if you can get paid for it) cite thoughts, beliefs, and assumptions as important mental processes that relate to anxiety.

Thoughts comprise the stream of mental events you experience as you go through the day. Many thoughts come as words, but thoughts can also come as images. You may say to yourself, "I'm so clumsy—I'll spill my drink," or you may picture yourself spilling a drink all over your white linen suit. Most thoughts are neutral ("I think I'll finish reading this chapter before I take a break"), but anxious thoughts are often negative ("If I take a break before I finish this chapter, I'll never get back to it, and I'll be shy for the rest of my life!").

Beliefs are the ideas and views that lie behind your thoughts. While most of us are aware of our religious and political beliefs, we may not be aware of some of our beliefs about social encounters. For example, some people believe they are unattractive. Others believe that people are always watching them and waiting to criticize their behavior. A small cadre of beliefs may form the basis of a multitude of thoughts. For instance, if you believe that others are always watching you, you will have many thoughts related to this belief when you are around other people.

Assumptions describe ideas about how one event relates to another in your picture of the world. Often these can be described using IF . . . THEN statements. An example of an anxious (negative) assumption is "IF I look nervous, THEN people won't like me." An example of a nonanxious (positive) assumption is "IF I look nervous, THEN people will accept me the way I am." An assumption often involves a prediction about the results of an action.

By paying attention to your thoughts you can often identify the beliefs and assumptions that lie behind them. Here are some examples:

Anxious Thoughts	Related Beliefs and Assumptions
Everyone will look at me when I enter the room. People will see how anxious I am. What if people think I look stupid?	People will watch me to see if I do something they can criticize or laugh at.
What if I say something stupid? What if I stumble on my words? What if I can't think of anything to say? What if I make a mistake when I'm talking?	I make more mistakes than other people. It's terrible to make a mistake. IF I make a mistake THEN people won't like me [or they'll laugh at me or criticize me].
I won't know what to say. People will find me boring.	IF I don't say something interesting THEN people won't like me.
My hair looks terrible. People will think I'm fat. Oh, no—I'm not as dressed up as the other people here.	I'm not as attractive as everyone else. IF I'm not really attractive, THEN people won't like me [or will criticize me or make fun of me].
I'm so nervous; I'll look like a real idiot.	IF I appear to be nervous, THEN people won't like me.

How do you change these negative thinking patterns? There are three steps in the process:

1. *Identify* the anxious thoughts, beliefs, and assumptions about social situations,

2. *Question* whether they are realistic and helpful,

3. *Develop coping thoughts* to deal with them.

Identifying Anxious Thoughts

You've already started to *identify* your anxious thoughts by completing the worksheet in Chap. 6 (Fig. 6.3). When you're beset by anxious thoughts, you tend to see things as more negative than they really are. Before the event, you may make negative predictions about how other people will respond to you, how you will perform, and how events will turn out. After the event, you may make negative evaluations of how you handled it. Certain patterns of anxious thinking are associated with social anxiety. Being aware of these patterns can help you identify them.

◆ *Perfectionism.* Most of us like to do things well, but some people are so focused on doing things perfectly that it causes a great deal of distress. If you are a perfectionist, you may spend much more time on an activity than is warranted, taking time away from more rewarding pursuits. Perfectionism can be particularly troublesome if someone is watching you. You may be so worried about making a mistake that you can't perform well. The most reliable way to avoid mistakes is not to do anything; many perfectionists become expert procrastinators who accomplish very little. Creative people allow themselves to make mistakes and learn from their mistakes as they go along.

◆ *All-or-nothing thinking.* Related to the problem of perfectionism is all-or-nothing thinking. When you think this way, if a social encounter does not go the way you wanted, you see yourself as a complete failure. A more constructive approach is to see where you have succeeded and consider where you can do even better in the future.

◆ *Catastrophic thinking.* This involves taking a disappointing experience and thinking it into a catastrophe. If you do not get that job offer (close that sale, get that date), you will never have another chance. In reality, most people have to put in a good number of job applications before they receive an offer.

◆ *Overestimating the danger in a situation.* Most of us know people who worried excessively about failing each exam despite their history of getting strong marks in all their courses. Likewise, a socially anxious person may expect social encounters to turn out badly, even though they often turn out well.

◆ *Underestimating your ability to cope with a difficult situation.* You may feed your anxiety by telling yourself that you will not be able to cope with a difficult situation. In reality, most people—including you—rise to the occasion when faced with challenging situations.

♦ *Interpreting anxiety as a sign of failure.* You may interpret your anxiety in a difficult situation as a sign of failure. Anxiety is a normal emotion. If you set out to accomplish a goal and achieve it, this is a success whether or not you were anxious during the activity. When climbers reach the summit of Mount Everest and then descend, they often feel sick and physically exhausted afterward. We do not see the climb as less of an accomplishment because of their emotional response.

♦ *Mind reading.* You may leave a difficult social situation thinking that other people reacted negatively to you. You may have seen a subtle sign that you interpreted as a negative reaction—a frown, a glance away, or a certain look in the eyes. Realistically, it is very difficult to know what another person is thinking without asking. Even couples who have known each other for many years often have to ask to find out what the other is thinking.

♦ *Negative bias in thinking about yourself.* You may emphasize your weaknesses and minimize your strengths. You focus on your negative experiences rather than the positive ones. You may use negative language such as "I'm a failure" or "I'm a loser" in describing yourself. Negative language is discouraging and tends to distract people from problem solving.

These are just a few of the patterns of unrealistic, negative thinking. There is no need to remember all the terms—just watch for these patterns when you are identifying your anxious thoughts.

Challenging Anxious Thoughts

Once you have identified your anxious thoughts in a difficult social situation, the next step is to *question* how realistic and helpful they are. Ask yourself:

♦ How realistic is this thought?
♦ What evidence do I have for this thought?
♦ Are there other ways of looking at this situation?

Developing *coping thoughts* follows naturally from questioning anxious thoughts and the resulting discussion you have with yourself. Coping thoughts help you see difficult encounters more realistically and suggest ways you can handle them. This is different than just using positive thinking. While coping thoughts are encouraging in tone, it is especially important to be realistic in sizing up the situation. For example, unless you are fabulously good-looking, rich, or a remarkable dancer (or all three), you would not want to develop a coping thought for parties that goes, "All the (wo)men in the room are dying to take me home." Similarly, you do not want to say to yourself, "I will not be anxious when I argue the case before the Supreme Court" when the reality is that you probably will be nervous. A more realistic thought for that situation might be, "I know my stuff, and I'm excited about this opportunity to show it."

People describe this approach as talking themselves through an anxiety-arousing situation. The best way to explain this process is with some examples of how people *identify* anxious thoughts and related beliefs, *question* and *discuss* how realistic the thoughts are, and *develop coping thoughts.*

▶*Anxious thought.* "Everyone will look at me when I enter the room."

Related belief or assumption. IF people watch me, THEN they will see me do something they can criticize.

Questions. *Are* people really watching me for something to criticize?

Is everybody watching me or are just some people looking at me?

How much of the time are they watching me?

Discussion. An alternative explanation is that most people watch others just to pass the time. Most reasonable people are not terribly critical. At any time, maybe a couple of people are looking at me; the rest are paying attention to other things.

Coping thoughts. "It's normal for people to watch other people. They usually get interested in something else after a few minutes."

"Most people are busy thinking about their own concerns. My situation will interest them for only a short time. I can handle it."

►*Anxious thought.*   "What if I stumble over my words?"

Related belief or assumption.   IF I make a mistake, THEN people won't like me [or they will laugh at me or criticize me].

Questions.   Is it true that people won't like me if I make a mistake? I don't criticize people when they trip over their words, so why would they criticize me?

Discussion.   People often stumble in conversation and no one seems to notice. Reasonable people realize it is normal to make an occasional mistake.

Coping thoughts.   "People make mistakes all the time when they talk. If I make a mistake I'll either correct it or just keep talking. That way the conversation will flow better."

"People don't care about these little slips."

"They won't think less of me if I make a mistake."

►*Anxious thought.*   "People will be able to see that I'm nervous."

Related belief or assumption.   IF I appear nervous, THEN people won't respect me.

Questions.   Can most people really tell if I'm nervous? Do people really react negatively if someone seems nervous?

Discussion.   People often can't tell if a person is nervous unless they ask. I have been nervous many times; people haven't seemed to notice, or if they did they didn't react much. Reasonable people accept how someone else is feeling.

Coping thoughts.   "It is best just to accept my nervous feelings. Most people won't react negatively."

"I'll just concentrate on what the other person is saying. People like a good listener."

►*Anxious thought.*   "I look fat!"

Related belief or assumption.   IF people think I'm overweight, THEN they won't like me [or will criticize me or make fun of me].

Questions.   Do people really care that much about how I look? Are others so bored with their own lives that they're concentrating on my weight?

Discussion.   Many people have trouble with their weight. Some people may react negatively, but those people are ignorant, and I won't pay attention to them."

Coping thoughts. "I can't worry about what every single person thinks of me. I'll just do my best to be positive."

"If I am a positive person, people will react well to me."

"If someone doesn't like my weight, that's his or her problem."

►*Anxious thought.* **"What if I can't think of anything interesting to say?"**

Related belief or assumption. IF I don't say something interesting, THEN people won't like me.

Questions. Do I really have to say something exceptionally interesting?

What if I just keep in mind a couple of questions to ask?

Discussion. I don't need to say brilliant things. A lot of conversations start with small talk about everyday matters. Being a good listener will help, too.

Coping thoughts. "I'll start with a question or two. Then I'll follow along depending on what the other person says."

"I'll listen carefully to what the other person says, and that will give me ideas for things to talk about."

►*Anxious thought.* **"What if she (or he) says no when I ask for a date?"**

Related belief or assumption. IF I get turned down, THEN it means no one would ever be interested in going out with me.

Questions. If I get one *no,* does that mean I will never get a *yes?* Just because this person might not be attracted to me, does that mean no one else will be?

Discussion. When you ask for a date, apply for a job, or try to make a sale, it is normal to get quite a few refusals. Successful people keep trying.

Coping thoughts. "When you ask for dates, it's normal to get refusals. Don't take it personally."

"Just stay friendly even though you got a *no, thanks.*"

"There will be other chances to ask someone for a date. Keep at it."

"It took a lot of nerve just to ask the question. Don't worry about getting some *no* answers along the way."

You can't change your pattern of anxious thinking with just one round of questions and coping thoughts. It is something you have to work on every day. If you practice developing and using coping thoughts regularly, you will find that your thinking pattern will change. As you try new ways of coping, you will also find that you gather new information to help question and counter anxious thoughts, beliefs, and assumptions.

Challenging Your Own Anxious Thoughts

In reading this chapter you have identified patterns of anxious thinking. Also, look back to the worksheets in Chap. 6. Now, on the worksheet in Fig. 7.2, list the social situations that are difficult for you and your anxious thoughts in those situations. Then work through the process of identifying related beliefs and assumptions, questioning them, and developing coping thoughts. We have allowed space for only four difficult situations. Make copies of the worksheet to plan for other difficult social encounters. As you continue to work on overcoming social anxiety, it will be helpful to return to these questions.

Coping Thoughts Worksheet

1. Difficult situation:

_____

Anxious thoughts:

_____

_____

Related beliefs or assumptions:

_____

_____

How realistic are these thoughts?

_____

_____

Figure 7.2 Developing coping thoughts worksheet.

Coping thoughts:

_____

_____

2. Difficult situation:

_____

Anxious thoughts:

_____

_____

Related beliefs or assumptions:

_____

_____

How realistic are these thoughts?

_____

_____

Coping thoughts:

_____

_____

3. Difficult situation:

_____

Anxious thoughts:

_____

_____

Figure 7.2   *Continued.*

Related beliefs or assumptions:

_____

_____

How realistic are these thoughts?

_____

_____

Coping thoughts:

_____

_____

4. Difficult situation:

_____

Anxious thoughts:

_____

_____

Related beliefs or assumptions:

_____

_____

How realistic are these thoughts?

_____

_____

Coping thoughts:

_____

_____

Figure 7.2 *Continued.*

Read over your list of coping thoughts and make sure you can use them in challenging situations. Practice saying them to yourself and imagine using them. The words should be your own, phrases you can hear yourself actually saying. At first, it may be difficult to recall your coping thoughts when you are anxious—that is, at the time when you need them most! Keep practicing, and with time your coping thoughts will seem very natural and come to you automatically.

Short List of Coping Thoughts

Many people find it helpful to write a short list of coping thoughts to use in challenging situations they frequently encounter. Based on the coping thoughts you wrote down on the worksheet in Fig. 7.2, now compile a short list of coping thoughts on the worksheet in Fig. 7.3. When you have finished your list, copy or rewrite it onto a small card and carry it with you. (If you have an electronic personal organizer, such as a Palm Pilot or similar device, you might also want to keep the list there.)

Coping thought 1:

_____

_____

Coping thought 2:

_____

_____

Coping thought 3:

_____

_____

Coping thought 4:

_____

_____

Figure 7.3   Short list of coping thoughts.

TIP: PRACTICE USING COPING THOUGHTS.

When some people consider coping thoughts they say, "I already know that. How is that going to help me?" Much of the information in coping thoughts may be knowledge you already have. The key to using coping thoughts effectively is to get in the habit of using them whenever you are anxious. The more you use them, the more readily you will be able to call them to mind when you need them.

Your Thought Diary

Now that you are aware of the role anxious thinking plays in social anxiety, you must use this knowledge in everyday life. A way to do this is to use a diary to keep track of both your anxious thoughts and your new coping thoughts (Fig. 7.4). Make copies of this diary to use as you work through the program in the coming weeks. Watch for times when you are feeling anxious before, during, or after a challenging situation. Make note of the date, the situation, the anxious thoughts that arose, and the coping thoughts you employed, and rate your anxiety on a 10-point scale from 0 (no noticeable anxiety) to 10 (as anxious as you ever get). This diary will help you identify anxious thoughts and see how consistently you are using coping thoughts.

Thought Diary

Date	Situation	Anxious thoughts, coping thoughts	Anxiety rating, 0–10

Figure 7.4   Thought diary.

CHAPTER 8

Taming Physical Symptoms

As we discussed in Chap. 6, physical symptoms are a normal part of the anxiety response, but they can be frightening. You may worry that others will notice your blushing, excessive perspiration, shaky hands, trembling voice, or noisy stomach. While these physical symptoms involve part of the nervous system that is not under direct voluntary control, there are a number of strategies you can use to indirectly influence them:

- *Acceptance.* By resisting physical symptoms of anxiety, you may increase them, whereas if you accept symptoms, you may actually reduce them. Your body's natural tendency is to return from an aroused state to a calmer state; it will get there sooner if you do not struggle against symptoms.

- *Refocusing.* Focusing your attention away from your symptoms and toward the external environment can help. For example, concentrate on the conversation you're involved in, rather than on your racing heart.

- *Coping thoughts.* These can help you both accept your symptoms and refocus your attention. Here is an example: "I'm really sweating a lot. Don't fight it. Just let it pass. Pay attention to the other person."

- *Plan what to say if someone comments.* You may be worried that someone will comment on a noticeable symptom ("Wow, you're sweating more than a pig at a luau, Hank!"). Most times, no one will say anything. But you'll feel less anxious if you are prepared with a good response. We'll discuss what you can say in these situations shortly.

- *Masking the symptoms.* Many people find they can conceal their anxiety symptoms. This can help you cope in the short term until the symptoms become less of a problem.

- *Relaxation.* Later in the chapter we will describe several relaxation strategies that can help reduce physical symptoms.

What If Someone Notices the Symptoms?

You may spend a lot of time worrying that someone will comment on your sweating, blushing, shaky voice, or noisy stomach. Ask yourself: "How often has someone commented on my anxiety symptoms?" This usually has never or only rarely happened. This is because the symptom may be obvious and important to you, but not to others.

Still, you'll feel better if you have a response ready. Here are a couple of strategies:

- When someone comments on your appearance ("You look a bit flushed, Miss Charlotte"), you do not owe him or her a detailed explanation, nor do you need to recount your life history. Keep your response short and sweet. Work out one or two phrases you would be comfortable saying.

- This may be a situation where it is appropriate to tell a *white lie*, provided it does not hurt anyone.

Let's return to several of the people we talked about in Chap. 6:

Nancy: "I wish I wouldn't blush!"

Nancy's blond hair, fair complexion, and tendency to blush made her worry about what people might say. She worked out a number of responses: "I'm finding it quite hot in here and I'm feeling a little flushed," or "I have really fair skin and it flushes easily." She could then direct the conversation toward another topic.

Michelle: "I can't stand this growling stomach."

Michelle, a dancer, was apprehensive about someone hearing her stomach growl. She came up with the following responses for when her stomach did its earthquake impression: "I guess someone is hungry down there," "I guess I shouldn't have skipped that meal," and "It sounds like the troops are restless." She could laugh and then move the conversation along.

Steve: "The sweating is so embarrassing."

Steve would always wear a bulky sweatshirt or sweater to hide the wet spots under his arms. Here are the responses he created: "I think my thermostat is turned up too high today (fanning himself)," "I don't know why I'm feeling so hot today," and "It seems really warm in here."

If you worry that others might comment on your symptoms, take a few minutes now to note each symptom and some responses on the worksheet in Fig. 8.1. Practice saying the responses until you remember them easily.

Masking Symptoms

Many people have discovered methods to mask uncomfortable and embarrassing symptoms. Steve learned to mask his excessive perspiration by wearing loose-fitting sweaters. Antiperspirants are available that can help reduce sweating for some people. Those with excessive perspiration in the hands can apply antiperspirant at night to reduce perspiration when shaking hands the next day. Those with excessive blushing may wear darker clothing that provides less contrast when the skin is flushed. People with excessive stomach activity sometimes obtain recommendations from doctors or pharmacists about medicines to reduce it. Each of these approaches can be useful, provided you do not use them as your only way of coping with anxiety. Once you broaden your range of coping skills, many of these masking approaches will no longer be necessary.

Symptoms and Responses

Anxiety symptom:

_____

Responses:

_____

_____

Anxiety symptom:

_____

Responses:

_____

_____

Figure 8.1   Anxiety symptoms and responses worksheet.

TIP: HOW MUCH DO YOU SAY? IT'S UP TO YOU.

A rule in most social situations is that *you* decide how much or how little information to disclose about yourself. When you arrive at work and someone asks "How are you today?" you are free to answer "Not bad," even if you feel upset about an argument at home that morning. On the other hand, you could answer, "Really stressed from an argument with one of the kids." It's totally up to you. This is not an issue of being honest or dishonest. Rather it is an issue of how much you want others to know about you.

Relaxation Strategies

Many of us experience a high level of muscle tension in everyday life. For some people, it is if they were working in a nitroglycerine factory. They are constantly looking for signs of an impending explosion and are ready to run for their lives at any moment. High levels of tension can also be related to a variety of health problems, including headaches and backaches.

Learning to relax when you are under pressure can help you perform more skilfully and quickly. Athletes learn that their performance is much smoother if they are able to relax their bodies and use just the muscles they need. Excessive tension leads to awkwardness and using more energy than you need to accomplish the task.

We will briefly review three relaxation approaches: *relaxed breathing, deep muscle relaxation,* and *imagery relaxation.* If you have already learned a relaxation procedure you find helpful, you may wish to continue using that one. But it can be useful to have a repertoire of relaxation strategies to use at different times and in different situations, so read on.

Relaxed Breathing

This is a simple technique that you can learn quickly. There is a tendency to breathe faster when you are anxious; this can lead to symptoms like dizziness or tingling in the hands, feet, or face. Relaxed breathing helps to bring these under control. One of the beauties of relaxed breathing is that you can use it anywhere without anyone noticing—in a parent-teacher meeting, standing in line at the grocery store, riding a bus, or at a bar mitzvah reception.

Start by observing your typical breathing pattern:

♦ Sit in a comfortable chair with armrests.

♦ Place your feet on the floor in front of you.

♦ Rest your elbows on the arms of the chair.

♦ Put one hand on your chest and the other on your stomach.

♦ Now close your eyes, and breathe in a way that feels natural to you. Let yourself be as relaxed and loose as possible.

♦ As your breathing settles down and you get into a comfortable rhythm, notice how much the hand on your chest moves and how much the hand on your stomach moves. Continue for a minute or two.

People often think that the chest muscles do most of the work of breathing. In fact, when you are relaxed the muscles of your diaphragm do most of the work. The diaphragm separates the chest cavity from the abdomen. It contracts and pulls down to bring air into your lungs and relaxes and moves back up to let the air flow out of your lungs. During relaxed breathing, your stomach moves out when you inhale and settles back when you exhale. There may be some movement in your chest muscles, but your stomach moves more. To confirm this, you may want to watch a sleeping child or pet (a cat or dog); when you do, notice how little the chest moves compared to the abdomen.

Now it's time to practice relaxed breathing. When you practice, make sure you are breathing at a relaxed pace (not too quickly) and allowing your diaphragm to do the work. Here's how to do it:

1. *Begin practicing in a quiet spot.*   Sit or lie in a place with good support for your back, neck, and arms.

2. *Breathe through your nose.*   Close your eyes and focus on your breathing. Breathe through your nose (if it's not blocked) at your usual rate.

3. *Breathe from your diaphragm.*   Let your stomach move out about an inch each time you inhale. When you exhale, your stomach will return to its resting position.

4. *Take long slow breaths, pausing for one second after you inhale and one second after you exhale.*   Remember, this is slow, relaxed breathing, not *deep* breathing, so take a natural amount of air, not a deep breath.

5. *Once you are in a comfortable rhythm, slow down the pace of your breathing.*   Find a natural and relaxed pace that feels comfortable.

6. *Imagine the tension flowing out of your body with each exhalation.* Many people find it helpful to imagine saying a word such as *relax* or *calm* each time they exhale.

7. *Keep up the practice for 5 or 10 minutes so you get used to the rhythm.*

Many people find they can learn the technique in a few sessions because it is simply breathing in a normal, relaxed way. Other people find it more difficult to settle into a relaxed rhythm. They find that they become uncomfortable when they focus on breathing. These people often breathe most irregularly in anxiety-provoking situations. If relaxed breathing is difficult for you, try to continue practicing until it becomes more comfort-

---

TRAP: **Don't focus on relaxation alone.**

Some people put too much emphasis on using relaxation techniques alone to reduce anxiety, without working on the other parts of the program. Relaxation works best when you use it consistently over time with other coping techniques, rather than just in the most challenging situations.

able. About 1 in 10 people never gets comfortable with the relaxed-breathing technique. If you're one of them, don't fret. Move on to one of the other techniques.

Deep Muscle Relaxation

This technique involves moving systematically through the muscles of your body, first tensing and then relaxing them, to release unnecessary tension. Start using the program outlined here:

1. *Begin practicing in a quiet spot.* Sit or lie in a place with good support for your back, neck, and arms. An easy chair or recliner is especially good. Do not lie down if there is a risk you will fall asleep before you have completed your practice.

2. *Tense each muscle group as described here for about five seconds.* Focus on the feeling when the muscles are tense. Then slowly release the tension. Feel the tension flowing out of the muscles as they become looser, heavier, and more relaxed. Let the muscle group stay relaxed for 10 to 20 seconds. Tense and relax each muscle group twice before moving on to the next group.

3. *As you release the tension in each muscle group, say the word* relax *slowly to yourself.*

4. *Notice how your muscles feel when they are tense and when they are relaxed.*

Now tense and relax each muscle group *twice:*

1. Clench your left fist; relax.
2. Clench your right fist; relax.
3. Bend both hands back at the wrists to tense the muscles in the backs of your hands and forearms; relax.
4. Clench both fists, bend your elbows, and bring your fists toward your shoulders to tighten the muscles in your upper arms; relax.
5. Pull your shoulders up toward your ears; relax.
6. Wrinkle your forehead and brow; relax.
7. Close your eyes tightly; relax. (Be sure to remove contact lenses first.)
8. Clench your jaw and teeth; relax.

9. Press your lips together tightly; relax.

10. Bring your head forward and pull your chin in toward your chest; relax.

11. Arch your back and stick out your chest and abdomen; relax.

12. Take a deep breath, filling your lungs completely, and hold it for five seconds; exhale and relax.

13. Tighten the muscles in your abdomen; relax.

14. Tighten the muscles in your lower back and buttocks; relax.

15. Stretch out both legs in front of you, pointing your toes; relax.

16. Tighten your calf muscles by flexing your feet and pointing your toes up toward the ceiling; relax.

After you have moved through all of the muscle groups, remain relaxed for two or three minutes with your eyes closed. Allow your body and your breathing to relax and focus on that feeling.

TIP: TAKE IT EASY ON THE TENSING.

Tense the muscles firmly, but don't overdo it. If you feel pain, cramping, or trembling, you are tensing too hard or too long (or both). If you have muscle or joint problems, you may wish to gently move or stretch that area rather than tense it, then relax it.

Most people find that if they practice this exercise daily for a week or two they are able to relax their muscles effectively. Once it is going smoothly, move through the tense-and-relax cycle more efficiently by using larger groups of muscles:

1. Hands and arms

2. Head, neck, and shoulders

3. Chest and upper back

4. Abdomen

5. Lower back and buttocks

6. Legs and feet

Once you have completed the tense-and-relax cycle, remain in place and allow yourself to stay fully relaxed for about 15 minutes.

TIP: MAKE TIME TO RELAX.

If, like most of us, you don't have 15 minutes to relax, then 10 will do. The important thing is to carve out *some* quiet time to practice relaxation. You won't be able to do this if the TV is blaring, the phone is ringing, your kids are yelling, and the dog is barking. Tell those around you, "I need 15 minutes alone in my room. Please don't bother me unless it's an emergency." Then go to your room, close the door, and don't emerge unless it's really an emergency.

After you have practiced the shorter list of muscle groups for a week or two and it is going well, move on to the simplest procedure of all: Tense your whole body for a few seconds and then relax, or take a long, slow breath and then relax your whole body as you exhale. Once you reach this level, you will be able to use the muscle-relaxation strategy at any time—at a social gathering, in line at the checkout counter, or even when you are riding a bike.

Check your muscle-tension level several times during the day. If it's high, take a minute or two to relax.

TIP: RELAX YOUR BODY TO REDUCE PAIN.

If you have frequent pain in your back, neck, or head, the tense-and-relax method (or frequent stretching and relaxing) may help relieve it.

Imagery Relaxation

Imagery relaxation—using your imagination to create a relaxing series of images—is a powerful method of focusing your attention. People who have difficulty with anxiety often form images of the many catastrophes that can happen. With imagery relaxation, you develop a detailed mental picture of a relaxing situation (or one you imagine would be relaxing). Think of vivid details and include as many of your senses as possible. What would you see, hear, smell, taste, and feel? Here is an example:

I'm sitting on a soft patch of grass at the side of a lake. It is evening, and the air is pleasantly warm against my skin. The sun is getting lower on the horizon, and the sky is starting to turn orange and pink. I can hear a motorboat in the distance. I can feel the moist air and smell the flowers. Birds are calling from the woods nearby. I am at peace.

Now get a piece of paper and write a vivid description of a relaxing scene you would like to use.

Imagine this scene during your imagery relaxation sessions. Allow yourself to think of other aspects of the scene and change it, as long as it remains relaxing. This technique can be especially helpful when you return home after a busy day or before you go to sleep.

Relaxation Practice

It is useful to familiarize yourself with more than one relaxation technique. Imagery relaxation works best during quiet periods or before you enter a challenging situation, whereas breathing and muscle relaxation are easier to use while the situation is happening.

Master one relaxation technique at a time. Practice every day until it becomes familiar. If possible, practice at first when you are not feeling tense. Then start using the technique when you are anxious. Once you have learned a technique, it will stay with you indefinitely, provided that you use it from time to time in your everyday life.

Relaxation Practice Diary

Use the relaxation practice diary in Fig. 8.2 to keep track of your practice (make as many copies of the diary as you need). After each practice session, record the date and time it occurred, where you practiced, how many minutes you practiced, and your tension level (on the 1 to 10 scale) at the start and end of the session. Finally, comment on how the session went.

TRAP: **Don't skip regular practice.**

Many people have difficulty making time for relaxation practice. Remember that a small time commitment to practice these skills regularly can save you time later. The benefits of relaxation may last for years after you master the techniques.

Relaxation Practice Diary

Date/ time	Where I practiced	Minutes spent practicing	Tension level— start	Tension level— end	Comments

Tension/Anxiety Rating Scale

None	Mild	Moderate	Severe	Very severe
0	1 2 3	4 5 6	7 8 9	10

Figure 8.2 Relaxation practice diary.

CHAPTER 9

Changing Your Behavior: Facing Your Fears

The Key to Conquering Anxiety

Facing your fear is the best way to overcome anxiety. The idea is not new. Most of us know the answer to the old question of what you should do if you fall off a horse. The correct answer is:

a. Shoot the horse.

b. Eat the horse.

c. Shoot the horse, then eat it.

d. Get back on the horse and ride again as soon as possible.

e. Sue the horse.

The correct answer, of course, is *d*. (Unless you live in France, in which case *b* is also acceptable, provided you've got the right wine.) Therapists routinely advise people to "get back on the horse" when they have experienced traumas such as motor vehicle accidents. The sooner you drive again, the sooner you will become comfortable with driving. The longer you avoid driving, the more your fear about driving will increase.

Using coping thoughts and managing physical symptoms won't be effective in the long run unless you also face your fears. Exposing yourself to your fear—or *exposure therapy,* as it is also known—is best accomplished step by step. This allows you to move ahead without having to endure situations where the anxiety is unusually high.

Avoidance Behavior Maintains Anxiety

We've talked about avoidance behavior, a strategy we learn early in life to keep ourselves out of uncomfortable or painful situations. We can hear you saying, "But I don't avoid many of the situations that make me anxious!"

Some people don't avoid anxiety-provoking situations, yet find their anxiety persists. Why does their anxiety continue even though they are facing their fears? The answer here often lies with more subtle types of avoidance. You may be physically present but still avoiding some important aspects of a situation. For instance:

- You go to school or work every day but avoid talking to certain people, such as fellow students you don't know well or the head of your department.

- In a meeting or class you avoid eye contact with the person in charge so she or he won't ask you a question.

- You avoid opportunities to go to coffee or lunch with your coworkers, or you go only with one or two you feel safe with.

- You listen to people discussing a topic you're interested in, but avoid giving your opinion because you are afraid of saying something foolish or stumbling over your words.

- You go to a social gathering only if someone you know well and trust is there with you. You rely on that person to do most of the talking.

- You meet one or two people at a gathering and spend the whole time with them. You do not make an effort to speak to other people.

- You spend a great deal of time preparing for all possible questions that could come up at a meeting or presentation.

- You go out to eat, but you avoid foods that are messy or easy to spill (such as soup or spaghetti with sauce).

- You worry about your hand shaking and spilling your beverage, so you order only those beverages with lids and straws.

In each of these cases, *subtle avoidance* prevents you from being fully involved in the situation. You are present, but you engineer ways of avoiding aspects of the situation you fear. This kind of avoidance limits the range of options and choices for your actions. You then continue to fear the situation because you worry, "What if my way of coping [avoiding] doesn't work?" You never develop confidence that you can handle the situation.

Roger: "I can't handle spontaneous conversation."

Roger was an experienced laboratory technician and president of his small union branch. He was often called on to speak at business meetings and participate in labor negotiations. To deal with his social anxiety, he had developed the strategy of being well prepared for meetings, bringing notes about issues he might have to discuss, and avoiding casual conversation that did not relate directly to those issues. But coffee breaks, lunches, and social gatherings were very difficult for him because he worried that he would not be able to think of what to say, as he wouldn't have a script. To overcome this aspect of social anxiety, Roger had to give up the subtle avoidance behavior of preparing notes and speeches for meetings and avoiding other conversation. He had to learn to trust that he would be able to make spontaneous comments, if necessary, and that he could respond to questions by saying he did not have the answer but would look into it.

Some people do have anxiety problems but no avoidance behaviors. For these people, it is usually anxious thinking that maintains their anxiety. If this is your situation, it is still important for you to face your fears. As you read this chapter, identify social situations that are difficult for you *even if you do not avoid them,* and practice going into those situations and using the coping techniques described in Chaps. 7 and 8.

Identifying Difficult Social Situations

You took the first step toward facing your fears back in Chap. 6, when you listed situations you avoid because of social anxiety. Return to that worksheet now, review your list, and add any others you may have forgotten. If you need more space, use more paper.

Now that you've reviewed your list, think about the avoidant behaviors

> **TRAP:** **Present in body but not in mind.**
>
> Another way to avoid being in an anxiety-provoking situation is to mentally avoid it. It is possible, for example, to be physically present at your office's holiday party, but wishing so hard that you weren't that you're really not there in spirit or in mind. Some people describe being in a fog throughout an event, able to think only one thought: "It'll be over soon. It'll be over soon." Others drink enough alcohol that they're out of touch with what's going on around them. These forms of cognitive avoidance—not being there in mind—have the same effect as other kinds of avoidance: they rob you of the opportunity to become comfortable in and confident about your ability to handle a situation. It is therefore important to focus on being in a situation: don't let your mind wander, make a point of consciously taking in your surroundings and other people, and let it sink in that you're actually there!

you've used to cope with these situations. There may be some situations that make you anxious which you don't avoid. You may be using some *subtle avoidance behaviors* in these situations to help yourself cope. Review the examples of subtle avoidance and list the ones you typically use on the worksheet (Fig. 9.1).

Situation   Subtle Avoidance Behavior

_____   _____

_____   _____

_____   _____

_____   _____

_____   _____

_____   _____

_____   _____

_____   _____

Figure 9.1   Subtle avoidance behaviors worksheet.

Developing Assignments to Face Your Fears

So far, you have identified situations that make you anxious, along with avoidance behaviors you use to cope with them. Now you're ready for the next step: giving yourself assignments to help you face your fears. To develop any new skill, you progress step by step, from where you are to where you would like to go. Your list of difficult situations will tell you where you are. The short-, medium-, and long-term goals you identified at the end of Chap. 6 will tell you where you would like to go. The best way to achieve these goals is to practice *facing your fears*. The more time you spend facing a fear, the more you will reduce it.

In the following section you will come up with ideas for *practice assignments*, social activities you would like to practice based on your goals. You should choose assignments that *are important to you, increase in difficulty*, and *are repeatable*.

Make the Practice Assignments Important to You

Start with assignments that matter to you and have some natural rewards built in.

Strong Assignment. If you are working toward being able to go to a fancy restaurant for your wife's birthday, "Eating in a restaurant with friends" would be a good assignment. The assignment would feel important, and there would be lots of natural rewards (enjoyable food and company) to keep you working at it.

Weak Assignment. If you are working toward being able to speak before a large audience but have no current need to do so, it would not make sense to choose "Speaking to a large group" right away. The assignment wouldn't feel important, and there wouldn't be any natural rewards to keep you going. You would probably feel that you were working hard to learn a skill you were unlikely to use in the foreseeable future.

Make the Practice Assignments Increase in Difficulty

Don't start with assignments that make you extremely anxious. Instead, start with assignments that make you somewhat anxious and over time move toward working on more difficult assignments. Remember, you've got to walk before you run. Start small and build on success.

Strong Assignment. If you ranked "Talking to a coworker at coffee break" as one of your easier short-term goals, that would be a good assignment to start with. You could test your coping strategies without feeling overwhelmed.

Weak Assignment. If you ranked "Giving a formal talk to a group at work" as the most difficult of your short-term goals, it would not be a good assignment to start with. You would probably feel overwhelmed by starting such a difficult assignment before you had successfully completed easier ones.

Make the Practice Assignments Repeatable

Pick assignments you can work on over and over again. Situations that you can control are best. Facing tasks that come up unexpectedly can help you overcome anxiety, but you cannot control when they will occur. They are difficult to practice frequently or regularly. Similarly, assignments that rely on unusual circumstances or other people are also hard to practice regularly. Assignments you can arrange every day or every week are especially effective.

Strong Assignment. "Making eye contact with people at work and around the neighborhood" is a good assignment because you can practice every day.

Weak Assignment. "Going to concerts" might be a difficult assignment to repeat if there aren't frequent concerts in your area (and if you aren't independently wealthy). This doesn't mean you shouldn't go to concerts, but you should also pick other repeatable assignments involving sitting in crowded places so you can practice frequently.

TIP: BUILD ENDURANCE.

Practice each assignment long enough that it has a chance to sink in. You may have attended a crowded meeting every Tuesday for the past two years and wonder why you're still anxious. The answer may lie in how long you spend in the situation. If you enter an anxiety-provoking situation and stay only a few minutes, it isn't long enough for your body and mind to adjust so that you feel more comfortable next time. How long is long enough? A minimum of 20 minutes—and preferably longer—each time you are in the situation should be long enough. For example, if you are practicing having coffee with colleagues, be sure you sit at the table with them for at least 20 minutes before you head off.

Your Practice Assignments

Now list some practice assignments you will be working on in the coming weeks on the worksheet that follows (Fig. 9.2). Consider the short-term and medium-term goals you chose in Chap. 6 and the difficult social situations you identified earlier in this chapter.

Practice Assignments

1. _____

2. _____

3. _____

4. _____

5. _____

6. _____

7. _____

Figure 9.2   Practice assignments worksheet.

Breaking Down Goals into Smaller Steps

Some of your short-, medium-, and long-term goals are activities you can start working on right away. Others may seem too complicated or difficult to launch into immediately. You can start working on these challenging goals sooner if you break them down into smaller steps.

♦ *Break down a complicated task.*   Having a group of family members, friends, or neighbors over for dinner may seem difficult. Start out by having one person over for coffee several times. Once you are more comfortable with this, have a few people over for coffee and a snack. Then start having one person for lunch or dinner, then a few people, and so on. (We were only kidding about serving horse and wine. Avoid horse altogether. For a list of mammals not to serve at social occasions, check out www.donteatme.com.)

♦ *Start practicing with just one or two people, then work toward larger groups.* If you have difficulty speaking at a large meeting, start by speaking informally at a small one, perhaps by asking a question. If you have trouble with conversations at large events such as wedding receptions, practice speaking to unfamiliar people at smaller events. For instance, have coffee with someone you don't know well at work or in the neighborhood.

♦ *Start by talking to people who are less intimidating, and work your way up.* Your goal may be to talk comfortably with your manager at work. If this is too difficult for a first step, you could start by talking with coworkers more often, then a supervisor, and then the manager. Talk about casual topics at first ("How was your weekend?") and move toward more substantive topics ("There's a problem I'd like to discuss with you").

♦ *Start out with casual situations and work toward more formal ones.* You may find it difficult to dine at fancy restaurants or business banquets. Facing less formal situations can help prepare you to face the more formal ones later on. One woman we know developed a strategy to overcome her restaurant anxiety. When she knew she had a meal coming up, she would find out where the event would be held and go alone or with a close friend to the restaurant for lunch or dessert well in advance of the event. This allowed her to become familiar with the layout of the restaurant and scope out the location of coat racks and restrooms. She was then better prepared when she went with a group. As she became more comfortable with eating in public, she no longer needed to visit the restaurant in advance.

Breaking Down a Difficult Task into Smaller Steps: Melissa

Melissa was a graphic designer and liked her job, but after two years in the same position she was still shy and nervous around her fellow workers. She did not go for coffee breaks, and she would eat lunch alone at her desk. She rarely spoke to coworkers unless they started the interaction. Her goal was to be able to talk with her fellow workers at coffee breaks and lunchtime. The idea of starting to do this seemed overwhelming to her. She decided to break her goal down into the following steps:

Step 1.   Make a short comment to a coworker at least once every morning and once every afternoon. Just make it small talk, such as "Hi, there," or "How was your weekend?"

Step 2.   When Step 1 is going well, go for three morning coffee breaks a week with the people that I know best. The first time, ask if I can join them for a coffee break. Just listen to the conversation and respond to questions.

Step 3.   Go for morning and afternoon coffee breaks at least three times a week.

Step 4.   At the coffee breaks, ask at least one question, or make one comment without being asked.

Step 5.   Go for coffee breaks and two lunches a week and make comments each time.

Step 6.   Go for coffee breaks and every lunch and make comments each time.

Step 7.   Go for coffee breaks and lunches and ask a question or make a comment to at least two people at each break.

Step 8.   Say yes and join in when colleagues invite me to a lunch or supper away from the office.

Melissa took each step over a period of several weeks, practicing a step repeatedly until she felt it was going well before moving on to the next one. She often felt anticipatory anxiety before practice sessions, but was surprised by how well they went. She was apprehensive when she moved to a new step, but before long she would feel more comfortable. Once her new way of handling coffee breaks and lunch became part of her work routine, she moved on to other goals.

Now review your goals to see which ones you would like to break down into smaller steps. Figure 9.3 provides forms for the first two goals. Make as many copies as you need to.

You're Allowed to Make Mistakes— Try It, You'll Like It!

A major factor that may influence your willingness to practice challenging situations is the fear of making mistakes. As we mentioned earlier, the most reliable way to never make a mistake is to avoid doing anything new. As people participate in social situations, it is normal to make mistakes. We can speak with some authority, because we are the world's champions at spilling coffee (usually all over papers at a meeting), tripping over words, mixing up names, and slamming into people in the hall. If you

Goal Worksheets

Goal: _____

Steps toward goal:

1. _____

2. _____

3. _____

4. _____

5. _____

6. _____

7. _____

8. _____

Goal: _____

Steps toward goal:

1. _____

2. _____

3. _____

4. _____

5. _____

6. _____

7. _____

8. _____

Figure 9.3 Goal worksheets.

develop a willingness to make mistakes, you will be able to be comfortable in a wide range of social situations. Here are some ways of handling mistakes:

- Burst into tears and run sobbing from the room. (We don't recommend this.)

- You can handle most slips of the tongue by either ignoring them or simply repeating the sentence and forging ahead. Do not spend a lot of time explaining or clarifying.

- Bumping into people can be handled with a simple "Sorry" or "Excuse me" and then getting on with things. If you bump into someone with a great deal of force, a simple "I'll be happy to pay for the surgery" should suffice. Again, keep it short and sweet.

- You can handle obvious mishaps such as spilling a cup of coffee by cleaning up and making a humorous comment such as "It's going to be one of those days," or "I guess this will ensure that I clean up my desk." It is best not to engage in excessive apologies or self-criticism. People appreciate someone who does not take himself or herself too seriously.

As you become more comfortable in social situations, focus on handling mistakes in a relaxed way with a good sense of humor. Some people who rarely make mistakes may benefit from making some and handling the situations effectively. Wouldn't it be an interesting experiment to intentionally spill a glass of water at a meeting just to practice handling it with humor!

TIP: REPEAT PRACTICE ASSIGNMENTS OVER AND OVER AGAIN.

Think of a skill you have learned over the years (for example, keyboarding, driving, or swimming). How many mistakes did you make as you learned? How many hours did you practice before you became good at it? Most of us have to practice the same activity over and over until it becomes an automatic part of our routine. In order to become comfortable and skilled in social situations, you must practice a great deal—the more frequently, the better. Focus on learning the new skill—not on avoiding mistakes.

Planning Practice for Each Week

As you face your fears, you should plan one week of practice at a time. First look over the sample weekly practice sheets in Figs. 9.4 and 9.5. You will notice that there are two steps. Sample 1 (Fig. 9.4) shows a week of pre-planned assignments. Sample 2 (Fig. 9.5) shows the same sheet a week later after it has been completed. (Note that an assignment has been added to Sample 2 that does not appear in Sample 1. Sometimes you'll decide to add a practice assignment after you've written in your first batch, or even do one spontaneously. This is fine!) Using the steps and assignments you just outlined, now turn to the blank weekly practice sheet (Fig. 9.6) and plan several assignments for the coming week (make as many copies as you want). Writing out your assignments makes it more likely that you will follow through.

As with your goals, your practice assignments should be specific and concrete so you can tell when you have completed them. There is space on the weekly practice sheet to keep track of the time you spend practicing each assignment over the week. We encourage you to spend several hours a week practicing. A few minutes a day just isn't going to do it.

Putting It All Together

As you work on your practice assignments, it is important that you use other coping skills as well. In challenging situations, remember to focus on other people and not yourself. Be aware of your anxious thoughts before, during, and after the situation and use the thought diary in Chap. 7 to work on coping thoughts. As you practice in more situations, you may discover new anxious thoughts and want to develop new coping thoughts to deal with them. Practice using the coping strategies in Chap. 8 to manage the level of physical symptoms you experience.

TRAP: **Don't be a hypercritical coach.**

You may tend to negatively evaluate your performance during and after challenging situations. This excessive self-criticism can discourage you from practicing. Cheer yourself on as you evaluate your efforts. Pat yourself on the back when you've taken a risk and done something difficult. And give yourself a break—don't expect perfection!

SAMPLE 1

Weekly Practice Sheet

Date: _June 10_ to _June 16_

Describe the assignments as specifically as possible in the spaces below. Try to say exactly what you plan to do. Draw a circle in the box for each day on which you plan to do an assignment; make more than one circle if you plan to do it more than once. Put a check mark in the circle when you do an assignment and note how much time you spent.

Practice assignments	Sun.	Mon.	Tues.	Wed.	Thurs.	Fri.	Sat.
Go for morning and/or afternoon coffee breaks with Fred. Ask a couple of questions.		◯◯	◯	◯	◯	◯	
Talk for a few minutes to coworkers outside of coffee breaks.		◯	◯	◯	◯	◯	
Invite neighbor to go for a walk.							◯
Phone Scott in Madison on Sunday.	◯						
Have sister over for dinner on Friday night.						◯	
Make eye contact and say hi to three people on the street Monday through Friday.		◯	◯	◯	◯	◯	

Total time invested in practice this week: _____

Figure 9.4 Sample weekly practice sheet 1: preplanned assignments.

SAMPLE 2

Weekly Practice Sheet

Date: __June 10__ to __June 16__

Describe the assignments as specifically as possible in the spaces below. Try to say exactly what you plan to do. Draw a circle in the box for each day on which you plan to do an assignment; make more than one circle if you plan to do it more than once. Put a check mark in the circle when you do an assignment and note how much time you spent.

Practice assignments	Sun.	Mon.	Tues.	Wed.	Thurs.	Fri.	Sat.
Go for morning and/or afternoon coffee breaks with Fred. Ask a couple of questions.		20 min / 10 min	20 min	No	10 min	20 min / 20 min	
Talk for a few minutes to coworkers outside of coffee breaks.		2 min	10 min	7 min	No	10 min	
Invite neighbor to go for a walk.							45 min
Phone Scott in Madison on Sunday.	20 min						
Have sister over for dinner on Friday night.						90 min	
Make eye contact and say hi to three people on the street Monday through Friday.		2 min 5 min	1 min	2 min 1 min 5 min	1 min 3 min 2 min	2 min 4 min	
Phoned Diane in Nashville on Thursday.					45min		

Total time invested in practice this week: ___5 hours, 57 minutes___

Figure 9.5   Sample weekly practice sheet 2: completed assignments.

Weekly Practice Sheet

Date: _____ to _____

Describe the assignments as specifically as possible in the spaces below. Try to say exactly what you plan to do. Draw a circle in the box for each day on which you plan to do an assignment; make more than one circle if you plan to do it more than once. Put a check mark in the circle when you do an assignment and note how much time you spent.

Practice assignments	Sun.	Mon.	Tues.	Wed.	Thurs.	Fri.	Sat.

Total time invested in practice this week: _____

Figure 9.6   Weekly practice sheet.

CHAPTER 10

Medications

There have been many breakthroughs in the treatment of emotional problems in recent years, foremost among them the development of new medications offering relief to persons suffering from anxiety and depression.

In this chapter, we review medications used to treat social anxiety and discuss their effects, possible side effects, advantages, and disadvantages. Whenever possible, we will refer to a medication by its generic, chemical name—for instance, acetaminophen—and, in parentheses, mention one or more of the brand names by which it is marketed (Tylenol). As we write this, paroxetine (Paxil) is the only medication approved by the U.S. Food and Drug Administration (FDA) for the treatment of social anxiety disorder. This means the FDA has evaluated the scientific studies that have tested paroxetine for its ability to ease symptoms specifically associated with social anxiety and found it to be effective for this purpose. However, evidence is emerging that other medications are also effective, and many of these are likely to be approved for social anxiety disorder in the near future. We will therefore cover these other medications here, too.

Please keep in mind that medications should be taken only on the advice of a licensed physician. A medical doctor is able to prescribe almost any medication for a particular condition (even if the medication is not FDA approved) if he or she has reason to believe it may be helpful.

Medications for Social Anxiety
in a Few Predictable Situations

There are basically two different ways to use medications for social anxiety. One way is to use them on an as-needed basis (the medical abbreviation for this is *p.r.n.*, from the Latin *pro re nata*). Only certain medications can be used this way. And they can only be used when the situation they are addressing arises occasionally and predictably.

Let's say Mark is socially anxious only in performance situations. Specifically, he is very uncomfortable speaking in front of a crowd. He avoids this whenever possible but has moved into a leadership role at work and is now expected to address the staff once a month. What is he to do?

First, we would recommend that he try a self-help approach. Or he could participate in a Toastmasters group or similar organization (see Chap. 5). Let's say he has already tried this, but found it hasn't helped much. He is looking for another way to cope with his public speaking anxiety. He would particularly like to be able to take something when he has to address the staff. What are his options?

Beta-Adrenergic Antagonists
(Beta Blockers)

This class of medications, sometimes known as *beta blockers,* can be useful on an as-needed basis for performance anxiety. Beta blockers used for performance anxiety include *propranolol* (Inderal and others) and *atenolol* (Tenormin). Beta blockers work by diminishing the effects of sympathetic nervous system stimulation. They are most commonly used for medical problems such as angina (chest pain caused by inadequate blood flow to the heart) and hypertension (high blood pressure). When used for these conditions, they reduce heart rate and lower blood pressure.

Beta blockers are thought to ease performance anxiety by reducing tachycardia (racing heart) and tremor (shaking). Some people with performance anxiety have a heightened awareness of these symptoms, which makes them even more nervous. By reducing some of these symptoms, the beta blockers can help people focus less on their bodies and more on the task at hand—in this case, speaking in public. Beta blockers are sometimes used by people in oral test-taking situations (medical students before their practical exams), and by concert artists to reduce their onstage jitters. Athletes such as archers and sharpshooters whose technique requires precise, controlled movements find that beta blockers improve their performance, presumably by reducing tremor. However, these medications are banned in some competitions of this kind.

Beta blockers are typically taken 30 to 60 minutes before a performance situation, as it can take this long for the medication to be absorbed and reach maximum effectiveness. A single dose will usually last for several hours, though this varies depending on the kind of beta blocker used.

Pros and Cons of Beta Blockers

Doctors often prescribe beta blockers for anxiety because they have prescribed them for other conditions, such as high blood pressure, and are familiar with their effects. But beta blockers are only modestly effective against anxiety, and generally inferior to other medications. In fact, the only clear indication for beta blockers in treating anxiety is for performance anxiety, and even then, they help only half the people who try them. When they don't work, other medications (such as benzodiazepines, described next) are often helpful.

A potential advantage of beta blockers is that they are not habit forming. They don't provide a feeling of euphoria, and it is impossible to become addicted to them. You can, however, experience withdrawal if you stop taking beta blockers suddenly. If you stop them abruptly—rather than taper them off slowly—after chronic use, your blood pressure could rise dangerously. So this class of medications, like all others, must be used under medical supervision.

Beta blockers used on an as-needed basis are generally well tolerated with few side effects. Occasionally, though, they can cause dizziness, lightheadedness, or fatigue. It is important to try the medication out on one or two occasions prior to the real performance situation to determine how it affects you and to find the right dose. You must do this, of course, under your doctor's supervision. When used on a regular basis (which is rare in the case of anxiety problems), they are more likely to cause fatigue and reduced capacity to exercise, as well as sleep problems. And they should not be used at all by people with respiratory problems such as asthma or chronic obstructive pulmonary disease (COPD); angle closure glaucoma (a form of high pressure inside the eye); or diabetes.

Benzodiazepines

Another remedy for performance anxiety is a class of medications known as *benzodiazepines*. Some benzodiazepines used on an as-needed basis for performance anxiety include *lorazepam* (Ativan) and *alprazolam* (Xanax). Benzodiazepines reduce anxiety by acting upon the so-called GABA-benzodiazepine-receptor complex in the central nervous system. Gamma-aminobutyric acid (GABA) is a naturally occurring anxiolytic (anxiety-reducing substance) in the brain. Benzodiazepines act in conjunction with GABA to further reduce anxiety. There is some evidence that people with anxiety disorders may differ from nonanxious people in the number or functional capacity of GABA receptors in the central nervous system. The theory is that benzodiazepines reduce anxiety by causing these receptors to function more normally. Theory aside, there is no question that benzodiazepines are extremely effective antianxiety drugs.

Like beta blockers, benzodiazepines can be used on an as-needed basis to treat performance anxiety, and are typically taken 30 to 60 minutes before the situation. Most of the time a relatively short-acting benzodiazepine such as Ativan or an intermediate-acting one such as Xanax is used for performance anxiety. The effects usually last several hours, depending on which one is used.

Pros and Cons of Benzodiazepines

Benzodiazepines are very effective and work quickly. They are also safe when used properly. These are their main advantages, and they are substantial.

Their main disadvantages, however, include the possibility of becoming physically dependent on them. Benzodiazepines can produce a feeling of euphoria, and are therefore liable to be misused by people who want to get a buzz. As a result, this class of medications has gotten a bad rap in the medical community. Although benzodiazepines are often an excellent choice to treat performance anxiety, they should usually not be taken by a person with a history of alcohol or drug abuse. There are exceptions to this rule, but someone with a tendency to abuse drugs or alcohol should try other medications first.

Side effects of benzodiazepines are generally few and mild. The main ones are drowsiness, sedation, and dizziness or lightheadedness, all of which often go away after a few days. Sometimes reducing the dose relieves these side effects. You must be careful when you use heavy or dangerous machinery, or when you drive, especially when first starting the medication or when the dosage is changed. Benzodiazepines should not be used in combination with alcohol, as they can intensify its effects.

Medications for Anxiety in a Wide Range of Social Situations

As we described earlier, many people are socially anxious in a wide range of situations—talking to groups of people, using the telephone, eating in restaurants, working while being observed, going to parties, addressing people in authority, writing in public places—that take place frequently or unpredictably throughout the day. For such people, a p.r.n. or as-needed medication is not a good choice, because they would need to take the medication repeatedly, often without sufficient warning to take it 30 to 60 minutes in advance, and would spend a great deal of time and energy worrying about when the right time would be to take it. For people with generalized social phobia, it's better to take a medication on a daily basis to prevent the occurrence of social anxiety symptoms.

Antidepressants

Antidepressants are among the most effective antianxiety agents. This sometimes confuses people who wonder, "I'm anxious, not depressed. Why is my physician recommending I take an antidepressant?" Although most of these medications were first tested and marketed for depression, recent studies show they are equally effective for anxiety, including social anxiety. Moreover, many physicians are familiar with them and comfortable prescribing them. Though some doctors may be relatively unfamiliar with social anxiety, they can translate their knowledge of how to treat depression with medication to the treatment of social anxiety.

Not all antidepressants can be used for social anxiety. Several that don't seem to be effective for this purpose are *bupropion* (Wellbutrin) and *desipramine* (Norpramin), and there may be others. Keep in mind that new medications come onto the market every year, so you and your physician should keep an eye out for new information that may become available after this book is published.

Selective Serotonin Reuptake Inhibitors (SSRIs). Selective serotonin reuptake inhibitors (SSRIs) comprise a class of antidepressant medications that came to the North American market in the mid-1980s. Serotonin, a chemical messenger in the brain, strongly influences mood and anxiety. SSRIs increase serotonin levels in the brain and are believed to relieve depression and anxiety through this mechanism.

The first SSRI to be marketed in the United States was *fluoxetine* (Prozac). It was soon followed by *sertraline* (Zoloft), *paroxetine* (Paxil), *flu-*

**TIP: AS YOUR CONFIDENCE RISES ALONG WITH YOUR MEDICA-
TION DOSAGE, PUSH YOURSELF TO DO MORE.**

Antidepressant medications work gradually and sometimes subtly. After several weeks of treatment, during which the dose is often increased by the physician to reach a therapeutic level (the dose at which it is likely to be effective), you may notice that you are less self-conscious, that you feel less like avoiding situations, or that you are simply more comfortable around others. When this starts to happen, it's your signal to start pushing yourself to do more and more. The medication should make it easier to do things you may have been dreading or avoiding for a long time, and it is important that you get out there and do them.

voxamine (Luvox) and, most recently, *citalopram* (Celexa). These medications have been shown to help reduce various forms of anxiety, including panic disorder, obsessive-compulsive disorder (OCD), generalized anxiety disorder (GAD), posttraumatic stress disorder (PTSD), and, of course, social anxiety disorder. Although some of these medications have been tested more extensively for one indication or another within this spectrum of anxiety problems, they are all probably effective for each condition. This means that if one SSRI doesn't work for you or causes bothersome side effects, you might find success with another one.

The SSRIs are not taken on an as-needed basis. Rather, they are taken regularly, usually once daily. Sometimes they are taken in the morning (as in the case of Prozac, which can disrupt sleep if taken too late in the day), or in the evening (as in the case of Luvox, which can cause drowsiness). Others, such as Paxil, Zoloft, and Celexa, are typically taken in the morning, but can be shifted to the evening if they cause drowsiness.

Pros and Cons of SSRIs. SSRIs are effective for a broad range of anxious and depressive conditions. This is a distinct advantage, as many people with social anxiety have associated problems with depression, and an SSRI is likely to treat both conditions.

SSRIs are generally well tolerated. This means that most people can take the medication, benefit from it, and put up with its typically minor side effects. In general, these can include sleep problems, drowsiness, lightheadedness, nausea or other gastrointestinal upset, and reduced sexual function. Most of these side effects diminish with time. But the sexual side effects—mainly difficulty reaching orgasm for women and delayed ejaculation for men, though diminished sexual desire and erectile problems can also occur—often do not diminish with time. As we mentioned earlier, if you have problems with side effects from one SSRI, you may have better luck with a different one.

SSRIs—and the other antidepressants we will be discussing in this section—take several weeks or even months to work. People do not feel less anxious after taking them for a day or two. This is very important to keep in mind. When you first take this type of medication, you will probably feel nothing other than perhaps some side effects. You must keep taking the medication with the knowledge that if it is going to work, it is going to take some time. You should not miss doses, as this can impede or disrupt the effects of the medication.

Monoamine Oxidase Inhibitors (MAOIs). A different group of antidepressants, the monoamine oxidase inhibitors (MAOIs), have been known for over two decades to be effective in treating social anxiety. MAOIs work by blocking an enzyme in the brain called monoamine oxidase, whose job it is to break down certain neurotransmitters—serotonin, noradrenaline, and dopamine—believed to regulate mood and anxiety (among other things). MAOIs block the effects of this enzyme, leading to higher levels of these chemical messengers in the brain.

The two most commonly used MAOIs in the United States and Canada are *phenelzine* (Nardil) and *tranylcypromine* (Parnate). Phenelzine has been more extensively studied for treating social phobia, though it is pretty clear that tranylcypromine is also effective. If one doesn't work or causes intolerable side effects, switching to the other might do the trick, although you must wait awhile—sometimes as long as two weeks—after stopping one before you start the other. And, of course, you should do this under a doctor's supervision.

Pros and Cons of MAOIs. MAOIs are among the most effective treatments for social anxiety. No study has yet been conducted to see if MAOIs are better than SSRIs, but some experts believe they are. There is no question that when these medications work—and they do work for more than 60 percent of patients who take them—they work extremely well.

The problem is that MAOIs can have a lot of side effects, certainly more than SSRIs. These include sleep problems, weight gain, sexual difficulties, and dizziness caused by low blood pressure when going from sitting to standing. This is one of the reasons why MAOIs are not usually the first choice for someone who is just beginning treatment. Rather, MAOIs are used when a number of other treatments have failed. We have seen them relieve social anxiety when nothing else has worked. So if you have tried several other treatments (medications and/or psychotherapies) and have not had a good response, you might ask your physician to consider an MAOI.

Another problem with taking an MAOI is that you need to eat a special diet. Some commonly consumed foods, including red wine and aged meats and cheeses, and some less commonly consumed ones, such as broad bean pods and Marmite (a vegetable extract popular in Britain), to name just a few, contain a chemical known as *tyramine*. If you are not taking an MAOI, the tyramine in these foods will not cause problems. However, if you *are* taking an MAOI, the tyramine in these foods can cause an abrupt and intense rise in blood pressure that can be extremely dangerous. It is therefore necessary to stick carefully to a diet low in tyramine if you take an MAOI. You can usually get a list of foods to avoid from your psychiatrist (an MAOI would rarely, if ever, be prescribed by a general practitioner), a dietician, or a pharmacist who is familiar with these medications. In the past, the MAOI diet was long and detailed and, consequently, very difficult to follow. Nowadays, most experts recommend a simpler diet that is easier to follow and still quite safe.

Reversible Inhibitors of Monoamine Oxidase Type A (RIMAs). We want to briefly mention another class of monoamine oxidase inhibitor: reversible inhibitors of monoamine oxidase type A (RIMAs). As we write this, RIMAs are unavailable in the United States, although one, *moclobemide* (marketed as Manerix), is available in Canada, Mexico, and many countries outside North America. Moclobemide has been shown to be effective for social anxiety in some studies and ineffective in others. Overall, moclobemide does not seem to be as effective as a regular MAOI (phenelzine or tranylcypromine), but it may be helpful for some patients. Its advantage over regular MAOIs is that no special diet is required. It also tends to have few side effects. When side effects do occur, they consist mainly of sleep problems, dizziness, and nervousness; most of these are transient.

Newer Types of Antidepressants. There are other types of antidepressants on the market at the time of this writing that are neither SSRIs nor MAOIs, and there will certainly be more to come in the next few years. None of these have yet been proven effective against social anxiety, though studies are ongoing for many of the medications we will mention here. Our experience suggests that at least some of these antidepressants will turn out to be useful in treating social anxiety.

♦ *Venlafaxine* (sold in an extended release formulation as Effexor-XR) is a dual serotonin and noradrenaline reuptake inhibitor (SNRI) that has already been shown to be effective for generalized anxiety disorder. It is a very effective antidepressant and has very few interactions with other medications. Its side effects can include sleep problems and occasional nervousness, but most people tolerate the medicine very well. It can also cause high blood pressure in a small percentage of people who take it (although only at the high end of the recommended dose range), so your physician needs to monitor your blood pressure as part of the routine of treating you with this medication. This medicine does not, however, cause the kind of abrupt, very large increases in blood pressure that can occur with MAOIs. Even though venlafaxine has not yet been formally approved for treating social anxiety disorder, most experts agree that it does work and are already using it. We prescribe venlafaxine for persons who do not respond to or have unpleasant side effects from SSRI treatment.

♦ *Nefazodone* (Serzone) and *mirtazapine* (Remeron) are other newer antidepressants on the market. Neither has yet been thoroughly evaluated for usefulness in treating social anxiety.

TIP: GIVE THE MEDICINES A CHANCE TO WORK.

Antidepressant medications usually take anywhere from four to six weeks to start working, and even longer—sometime three or four months—to reach their maximum effect.

Be patient! Think about how long you've lived with your symptoms. The wait will be worth it.

Benzodiazepines for Generalized
Social Phobia

We discussed benzodiazepines, taken on an as-needed basis, earlier in the context of performance anxiety. This class of medications also can be used to treat generalized social anxiety disorder. When used for this purpose, benzodiazepines are taken on a daily basis, rather than on an as-needed basis. The reason for this, as we mentioned earlier, is that if you experience social anxiety in different kinds of situations—many of them unpredictable—it doesn't work to take a medication on an as-needed basis, because you wind up needing it many times a day, and you don't have 30 to 60 minutes' advance warning.

Studies show that two benzodiazepines, *alprazolam* (Xanax) and clonazepam (*Klonopin*), reduce social anxiety when taken regularly. Alprazolam is usually taken three or four times daily, whereas clonazepam, which stays in the bloodstream longer after each dose, is usually taken once or twice daily.

Although some doctors believe that benzodiazepines can be used as a first-line treatment for generalized social anxiety, we prefer to reserve this class of medications for people who don't do well on an SSRI or other antidepressant. In these cases, we will sometimes add a benzodiazepine to an antidepressant to achieve a better overall effect. At other times, we may use a benzodiazepine alone.

The pros and cons of benzodiazepines taken on an as-needed basis also apply here. People with drug or alcohol abuse problems should take benzodiazepines only when other treatments have failed and, even then, only under a doctor's close supervision.

Note: *Buspirone* (BuSpar), a medication often prescribed for generalized anxiety disorder, seems *not* to be effective for social anxiety disorder. Buspirone belongs to a class of medications called *azapirones*.

Other Antianxiety Medications

Doctors are starting to prescribe several other classes of medications to treat social anxiety. These include a medicine from the class known as *anticonvulsants* (used to treat seizures), and medicines from the class known as *antipsychotics* (used to treat psychosis). It is not unusual for a medication developed for one condition to turn out to be useful for others. Other examples include blood pressure medicines turning out to be useful for preventing heart attacks, and pain medicines such as aspirin turning out to be useful for preventing strokes.

An anticonvulsant named *gabapentin* (Neurontin) has shown some promise as a treatment for social anxiety disorder. It may turn out to be a popular form of treatment, because it has very few interactions with other medicines, and it may be less addictive than benzodiazepines (though this remains to be proven). And several new antipsychotic medications, including *olanzapine* (Zyprexa) and *risperidone* (Risperdol), are showing some potential for people with social anxiety who are resistant to other forms of treatment. Although this information is quite preliminary, we provide it so you can keep an eye out for future developments and discuss them with your physician.

TIPS

♦ Sixty to seventy percent of people with social anxiety disorder will respond well to an antidepressant or benzodiazepine.

♦ People who don't respond well to their first medication may have a better response to a different one.

♦ Sometimes several different medications must be tried before the best one is found.

♦ Medications are sometimes combined to achieve a better overall effect.

Herbal and Other "Natural" Remedies

Trying herbal or other natural remedies to help reduce anxiety has become extremely popular. A recent Canadian study showed that more than half of people with social anxiety had tried one or more of these alternative therapies. You may have read about *St. John's wort,* an herb that is being studied to treat depression, or *kava kava,* which is purported to have antianxiety properties. Although we hope that research may lead to the discovery of safer, more effective, and better tolerated treatments for anxiety, we warn you that the scientific evidence that these treatments work is sparse indeed at the present time.

You may nonetheless be tempted to try one of these naturopathic remedies before you try traditional medical therapy. If you do, we advise you to buy the product from a reputable dealer and to discuss its use with your physician before you use it. It is particularly important that you do so if you suffer from any serious medical conditions, or if you are taking other medications. Even though these substances are marketed as natural, they may indeed have physiological effects and can interact adversely with other medicines you may be taking.

Getting the Most Out of Your Medication

Here are some pointers to help you get the most out of the medication you take for social anxiety and related problems.

Understanding and Dealing with Side Effects

The kinds of medications most commonly used to treat social anxiety—antidepressants and benzodiazepines—are generally very safe and very well tolerated. But any medication can cause side effects. These are usually most noticeable when you first start taking a medication or when the dosage is increased. Most side effects of these types of medications diminish or disappear with time. Your doctor may also be able to suggest ways to minimize some side effects. For example, if you are taking the medicine in the morning and feeling drowsy during the day, you might be able to take the medicine at bedtime instead. Some side effects, such as those affecting sexual response, are less likely to diminish with time and are often difficult to treat (although they go away when the medicine is stopped).

If you feel you can put up with a medication's side effects, do so, and give it a chance to work. Once you have been taking a medication for awhile (usually several months), you can judge whether it's worth putting up with its side effects to enjoy its benefits.

But how do you know if a side effect is serious? How do you know when to mention it to your doctor?

If you read the package insert, you are likely to see a list of every side effect known to human science. This can be very scary. It is important for you to realize that the pharmaceutical companies have an obligation to report any side effect associated with the medication, even if it is extremely rare.

You are not likely to be interested in knowing what kinds of side effects occur in 1 in 10,000 people. You want to know about the *common* side effects, or what kinds of side effects occur in more than 5 or 10 percent of people who take the medication. This information is usually available in professional books such as the *Physician's Desk Reference* (*PDR*) or other printed or Internet-based resources. Look for reading materials and Web sites designed for consumers. These usually list common side effects so you can assess the kinds of problems you may encounter when taking a new medication.

Having said this, it is also important for you to know that any medication can cause almost any side effect. For example, 1 in 1 million people might develop fuzziness of the eyebrows when taking the fictional medication Vaysnischt. You could turn out to be one of those people—although, of course, the odds of this happening are very low (1 in 1 million, in this case). So you've taken this new medication, and you're sitting at home mowing your eyebrows and wondering, "Could this be due to the medication? Should I call my doctor?" The answer is absolutely *yes!* This is essential, of course, should you experience breathing problems or develop a rash or other symptoms that lead you to believe that you might be having an allergic or other serious reaction.

If you are experiencing anything unusual, frightening, or just plain worrisome, call your doctor. It is important that you feel comfortable taking a medication, and you can't feel comfortable if you are uncertain of how safe it is. Don't worry about bothering your busy doctor. This is part of his or her job. Most doctors would very much prefer that patients call with questions, rather than stop taking the medication and delay their recovery. If your doctor is too busy to answer your questions, find another doctor.

Medication Dosages

Different medicines have different dosages. For example, consider two medications for pain, Indocid and Tylenol. A typical adult dose of Indocid is 50 mg, whereas a typical adult dose of Tylenol is 500 mg. Does this mean that a dose of Tylenol is 10 times as strong as a dose of Indocid? No; 50 mg of Indocid and 500 mg of Tylenol are equivalent in their ability to block pain.

The actual dosage number—5, 50, or 1000 mg—means nothing when you're comparing different medications. It's like comparing apples and oranges. Dosage *does* mean something, of course, when you're talking about a particular medication. For example, 1000 mg of Tylenol delivers twice as much acetaminophen (the active ingredient) as 500 mg of Tylenol.

So don't be frightened if your friend is taking 20 mg of Paxil and your physician suggests you take 75 mg of Effexor-XR. Your medication isn't any stronger. It's just a different medicine with a different dose range.

Keep in mind that treatment for anxiety problems usually begins with low doses—doses we know are usually too low to actually work well—and then increases over several weeks or months until the therapeutic dose is reached. We start with low doses and increase slowly to minimize side effects. Also keep in mind that some people will do well with lower doses and others will need higher doses. This doesn't have as much to do with the severity of the anxiety as it does with the different ways people react to medication.

Table 10.1 lists some medications commonly used for social anxiety, along with usual dosages.

Making Your Medication Work for You

A medication for social anxiety can help you in many ways. It can help reduce your anxiety in new situations. It can make you feel more comfortable around people you don't know well. It can make you feel less self-

TABLE 10.1 Medications Commonly Used to Treat Social Anxiety

Medication	Brand name	Dosage, mg/day*
Antidepressants		
Fluoxetine	Prozac	20–80
Fluvoxamine	Luvox	100–300
Paroxetine	Paxil	20–50
Sertraline	Zoloft	50–200
Citalopram	Celexa	20–60
Venlafaxine	Effexor-XR	75–225
Phenelzine	Nardil	45–90
Benzodiazepines		
Alprazolam	Xanax	2–6†
Clonazepam	Klonopin	1–4

*Some persons will require higher or lower dosages than those listed here.
†Total daily dosage divided across 2–4 doses per day.

> **TRAP:** **Medications can interact with one another in unwanted ways.**
>
> It is important that you tell your doctor (and the pharmacist who is filling your prescription) about any and all medications you are taking. This includes over-the-counter medications such as painkillers, sleeping aids, and cold remedies—even vitamins and nutritional supplements—as well as herbal and naturopathic substances.

conscious. It can also help reduce depressive symptoms that so often go hand-in-hand with social anxiety.

But you can't just sit back and wait for the medication to do it all. In our experience, the people who tend to do best are those who push themselves to do the most while they are taking the medication. As soon as the medication starts helping them, they begin to practice doing things they have avoided in the past. They push themselves to talk to people, to take courses, to invite friends over for dinner—anything to give them a chance not only to see if the medication is working, but also to improve their confidence.

So if you find that a medication is making you feel less socially anxious, don't stop there. Invest some time in your self-help program. You'll be glad you did.

CHAPTER 11

Helping the Shy Child

Shy children are often delightful. They are quiet, obedient (well, sometimes), and rarely get in the way. Teachers love them, though they don't always know that social anxiety is the reason for their silence and compliance. Parents are more likely to be perturbed by their children's shyness. Like the time Marisa hid behind the couch when the Wolfs came over for dinner. The Wolfs thought it was adorable (or at least they said so). Mom and Dad were, frankly, annoyed. They'd tired of this behavior. It was kind of cute when Marisa was age 3, considerably less so now that she was 9.

Shyness, of course, begins early in life. Parents of shy children recognize the signs very early on. Sometimes the child will be excessively anxious around strangers or will avoid new situations. Marisa's parents found that she wouldn't climb the ladder to the playground slide without help. Her peers, on the other hand, couldn't wait to get out of their parents' reaches the moment they reached the playground. As Marisa grew, this fear of novelty showed itself primarily around new people. Marisa wouldn't say hello to children she didn't know, and would hide behind her parents' legs when introductions were made. With time, she did warm up and play with other children. But it was extremely difficult for her to approach new playmates or initiate a conversation or game. Her parents worried about this behavior, but Marisa was otherwise a well-adjusted little girl, so they didn't do anything about it.

Are You Overreacting?

Parents sometimes think they may be overreacting when they express concern over a child's shyness. It is our experience that the feedback parents get from professionals often reinforces this view. Teachers, who are often expected to function as educators, counselors, nurses, and disciplinarians, may be too busy trying to put out fires ("Tommy, give Teresa back her Ritalin and stop jumping on the computer!") to concentrate on a well-behaved, quiet child. If the child is not causing problems in class, this may be viewed as a blessing, not something that requires intervention. Only if the child is behaving in a way that is unacceptable to the school milieu—for example, being absolutely silent even when called upon—is the teacher likely to call the school psychologist. Even then, most school psychologists have relatively little experience helping shy children.

Similarly, most pediatricians have limited experience and time to deal with shyness and social anxiety. Many pediatricians, it should be noted, have considerable expertise when it comes to behavioral problems such as attention deficit disorder (ADD) and related issues such as learning difficulties. Few, however, have experience helping parents who are concerned about an introverted child. The tendency, then, is for doctors to dismiss parents' concerns about a child's shyness.

If you are concerned about the extent of your child's shyness, chances are you are *not* overreacting. You may be made to feel this way, but don't be easily assuaged. Chances are good that, by the time you've reached this point in the book, you know a lot more about shyness and social anxiety than other people do, including most teachers and doctors! This, fortunately, is changing, as word gets out about the potential seriousness of untreated social anxiety. But you need to be a strong advocate for your child's needs. If you feel there's a problem, don't accept the all-too-common answer, "It's just shyness. It'll go away."

Fortunately, there are many things a parent can do to help a child overcome social anxiety. In most cases, professional help is not required. We advise parents to work with their child to make him or her more confident in social situations. (We give examples of what to do a little later in this chapter.) Yes, there are children who will outgrow it on their own, but it is difficult to know if your child is one of them. Implementing a plan to help a child become more socially confident is a lot like planning an exercise program. Yes, most children will run around on their own and get plenty of exercise (although television, video games, and home computers make this less certain nowadays). But some children will become couch potatoes if left to their own devices. They need more of a push. By involving them early and regularly in team and individual sports, during and/or after school, we ensure that our children get enough exercise. We need to do the same thing with shy children when it comes to getting enough social exercise.

What Can You Do to Help?

It can be very difficult to watch your child endure social situations that cause so much distress. The inclination is often to protect children from feeling bad by removing them from the situation or stepping in to make it better. For example, when Marisa hid behind her mother's legs rather than say hello to a new child, her mother would say, "Marisa is just a little shy. She is very happy to meet you, though!" Or when Bryan felt afraid at his friend's bowling party, his father took him home only minutes after they arrived. Although parents do this with the best intentions, it is almost always a bad idea. By stepping in to make things right—by speaking for your daughter or making it easy for your son to leave an uncomfortable situation—you wind up reinforcing your child's fears.

Having read this far, you know about the importance of exposure, of facing your fears gradually and repeatedly until the anxiety associated with the situation loses its intensity and fades away. This principle applies to children as much as it does to adults. The difference, of course, is that parents are in a position to help—or inhibit—their child's exposure to anxiety-provoking situations. When children are very young, particularly prior to age 8 or 9, you have a lot of power to guide them in the right direction when it comes to increasing their social confidence. As they become older, particularly when they become teenagers, parental influence is often less intense. Teenagers, as anyone who has ever encountered one knows, don't like being told what to do. Consequently, parents need to figure out ways to help their teenagers without getting into a power struggle with them.

This is a very important aspect of helping a child of any age—knowing how much to push, and finding ways to get the child to buy in to the program. In our experience, this is the piece of the puzzle that parents often have the most problems with. Children will usually resist doing things that make them uncomfortable, and telling them that it is for their own good rarely works. We have found that parents who spend time explaining the plans to their children beforehand tend to experience the least resistance. Depending on the child's age and level of understanding, this explanation may vary. For some, the explanation will present the need for "practice—like riding a bike. In the beginning it can be scary, and I'll be there to help you. As you get better at it, you'll do more and more of it alone." For older and more sophisticated children, an explanation of the importance of exposure can be both satisfying and motivating.

Are You Pushing Too Hard?

Most of the time a parent can do a wonderful job helping a child overcome shyness and social anxiety by using the strategies we offer. A reason to seek professional help would be if you find yourself getting into power struggles with your child, and don't know if you are pushing too hard or not hard enough. For example, if your 16-year-old daughter has never been to a school dance but professes disinterest rather than fear, it can be hard to know what to do. An experienced mental health professional can work wonders here. School counselors and psychologists, in particular, are usually very good at helping out when these kinds of conflicts arise between parent and child. Even if they don't have much experience with social anxiety, they should be able to help you implement a plan based on the strategies outlined in this book. In fact, if you do enlist the assistance of a therapist, you may wish to recommend that he or she read the book! Most counselors are grateful to have the chance to learn something new.

Tailoring a Self-Help Program to Young Folks

The principles for overcoming social anxiety you read about earlier apply to young people, too. Your job as a parent is to provide support:

♦ Motivate your child to work on overcoming social anxiety.

♦ Provide your child with opportunities for exposure.

♦ Provide your child with encouragement and praise when he or she succeeds.

Here are some ways you can implement an exposure plan with your child:

♦ *Be a coach.* When an opportunity presents itself for your child to say something to another child or an adult, encourage him to speak up. For example, when you order food at a restaurant, ask your son to order for himself. (Let him practice with you beforehand—you can role-play that you're the waiter or the counter attendant.) If he whispers, ask him to speak up. If he refuses, ask him to order dessert for the family later in the meal. If he can't do it the first time, don't get angry. Praise him for trying, and let him know that you're going to keep on urging him to try. (Don't withhold the dessert! The reward is for effort, not for success!) Let your child know you're not going to give up, and you're sure he'll be able to do it soon.

Rewards can help motivate many children to tackle tough situations. If possible, tie the reward directly to the behavior: "Tina, you may have a cookie if you go up to the counter, order it, and pay for it yourself." For older children, the reward can be a fun activity that itself promotes further interaction with peers: "Erin, if you invite a friend over on Saturday evening, we'll get pizza and a video." With time, your child will keep on doing these things not just for the material payoff, but because it feels good to be confident!

♦ *Be a matchmaker.* Provide opportunities for your child to interact socially with other children. Sometimes socially anxious children don't want to play with other kids, and they can come up with some very creative excuses. Let your child know that having friends is an important part of life. Make it a priority. Invite another child to tag along with you and your daughter, and encourage her to make conversation, to express her feelings, and to make the other child feel welcome. Encourage your daughter to invite her peers to hang out at your house. This can provide her with an opportunity to gradually warm up to new friends (and, particularly in the case of an adolescent, under your watchful eye). Once again, praise her for these positive behaviors.

♦ *Set an example.* Teach your child how to handle social situations. The best way to do this is not by telling, but by showing. And the best way to show is to let your child see you do things regularly in your everyday life. Let your child see you look someone in the eye, firmly shake hands, and say "Pleased to meet you." It can also be useful to talk out loud (to yourself, but knowing your child is listening) about how to approach a challenging social situation. For example, while getting dressed to go out to a business dinner, you might say, "I'm going to be meeting some new people tonight. I'll be sure to say hi to everyone, even if I don't remember all the names later."

Advice for Teachers

If you are a teacher, you are in a great position to help. What can you do? First, you can push for the school psychologist to work with the child. Too often, shy children don't get this opportunity because counselors are overburdened with caseloads of children with "more important" problems (such as the 11-year-old cherub with a proclivity for firearms). Quiet, socially inhibited children often wind up neglected because school resources are limited, and the squeaky wheel all too often gets the grease. As a teacher, you are in the best position to make sure that a shy child gets the help he or she needs.

You can also implement classroom procedures designed to benefit shy children. Talk with the children beforehand, and warn them that you intend to call on them to answer questions and speak before the class. You may wish to coach them ahead of time so they know the answers. Let the children know that the goal is for them to become more comfortable speaking out loud, not to embarrass them—and not, at this point, even to see if they know the answer. Remind them that with practice, speaking in class will become easier and easier. Be careful not to draw undue attention to these children; ask other children to perform from time to time.

In fact, you may wish to incorporate public speaking into your curriculum—if you haven't already done so. Educators seem to have caught on to the importance of learning public-speaking skills and developing confidence in this area, and they are requiring their students to do many more oral presentations than was the case a generation ago. This is a great advance. If your school is behind the times, be the one to bring it up to date about the merits of providing opportunities for children to speak before their peers.

Medications for Children and Adolescents with Social Anxiety

When self-help and psychological interventions are not doing the job, you may want to consider medication. There is growing evidence that the same kinds of medicines used to treat generalized social anxiety disorder in adults can be safely and effectively used for children.

There are several reports in the medical literature about using the benzodiazepine class of medications (for example, clonazepam [Klonopin]) to treat severe social anxiety and/or selective mutism in children. But the most exciting advances in this area come from studies of children and adolescents who have been treated with selective serotonin reuptake inhibitors (SSRIs; for example, fluvoxamine [Luvox], citalopram [Celexa], and paroxetine [Paxil]). These studies show that children with social anxiety disorder—as well as those with separation anxiety and generalized anxiety, which frequently cooccur with it—can be safely and effectively treated with SSRIs, as can adults.

Most parents would prefer to try nonmedication approaches first. We assume you will have first attempted to use self-help techniques or will have worked with a school counselor, psychologist, or pediatrician to deal with the problem. If these approaches have failed or been only partially successful, you would be wise to seek medical help.

Where do you go to get medication for your child or adolescent? Doctors are increasingly prescribing SSRIs for young people, but finding the optimal dose and dealing with side effects can sometimes be more challenging than with adults. You therefore want to find someone experienced at prescribing these medications for children and adolescents. If you have worked with a school counselor or psychologist, he or she may be able to recommend the name of a psychiatrist who specializes in young people.

An alternative would be to talk with your family doctor or pediatrician. He or she may have experience in using these medications with children and adolescents, and may feel comfortable providing the treatment. If not, he or she should be able to refer you to an appropriate psychiatrist in your area.

TIP: IF MEDICATION IS HELPING YOUR CHILD OR ADOLESCENT, DON'T STOP THERE.

As the medication begins to take effect, encourage your child to do things that he or she has avoided in the past. If your teenage daughter has declined a classmate's invitation to get together, urge her to call the classmate on the phone and invite her over to the house. If your 9-year-old son watches from the kitchen window as the neighborhood kids play street hockey after school, help him get his skates on and urge him outside. Provide your children with opportunities to speak to new people: ask your daughter to ask the waitress to please bring water to the table; invite your son downstairs to say hello when company arrives (and ask him to stay long enough to participate in the conversation); suggest to your daughter that she phone the movie theater to find out what's playing and when. Remember, medication will reduce social anxiety, but it will not build social confidence. That will come only with practice.

Part Three

Improving Your Relationships

CHAPTER 12

Polishing Your People Skills

Having good people skills—knowing how to act and what to say in a variety of situations—can be priceless. Although some people are more naturally adept at this than others—we might call them more socially athletic—almost anyone can improve his or her level of social proficiency. Neither of us is a gifted physical athlete, but we ride bikes, swim, and play tennis well enough that we don't look like total klutzes. Moreover, we have developed our physical athleticism to the point that we can not only do these things, but also actually *enjoy* doing them!

Becoming more socially athletic is not much different from becoming more physically athletic. First, the goal is not to become a social Olympian— the life of every party, the envy of every Toastmasters group. The goal is to become socially proficient enough that you can hold your own at a cocktail party or business meeting and feel good about the experience. Moreover, having good people skills can help refocus your attention away from concerns about your own anxiety reactions and what other people may think about you.

In this chapter, we talk about people skills that are useful in a variety of social situations. Think of these skills as ways to improve your social athleticism. Some of the situations we discuss may not be at all difficult for you. In that case, skim the material quickly. Other situations may be more formidable for you; read this material more carefully.

Eye Contact

Many people with social anxiety have difficulty making eye contact. It is important that you be aware of this, because eye contact is a critical part of interpersonal communication.

Eye contact is important throughout the animal world. In colonies of monkeys and baboons, the dominant animal makes eye contact and the submissive animal looks away. Among humans, different cultures have different customs about eye contact. It was only when scientists studied people's behavior during conversations that they were able to state what the rules of eye contact are in European and North American cultures. We tend to learn these customs incidentally as we grow up; no one gives us lessons in eye contact. Nonetheless, it is easy to learn the rules and, with practice, become proficient at using eye contact to enhance your personal interactions.

TIP: LEARN THE RULES FOR EYE CONTACT.

When someone is speaking, look at that person, whether you are in a group or in a one-to-one conversation. This indicates that you are listening. When you are speaking one-to-one, vary the eye contact, with periods of direct contact (about half the time) alternating with short periods of looking in the general direction of the other person but not making direct eye contact. This takes on a rhythm of making eye contact for a few seconds (somewhere between 2 and 10), then looking away, then making eye contact, and so on. When you are speaking to a group, make eye contact over time with most or all of the people in the group; you should be making eye contact with someone most of the time. Eye contact allows you, the speaker, to see the reactions of those who are listening and permits them to show a reaction to what you've said.

Different cultures may have other rules of eye contact. For example, in some cultures it would be considered rude if a young person made a lot of eye contact with an elder when the elder was speaking. When you are in a situation involving people from another culture it can be interesting to observe the unwritten rules about eye contact. If you plan to conduct business in another country, it is critical that you learn about that culture's rules of eye contact—and other parts of social discourse—before you get on the plane.

If eye contact is difficult for you, practice following the *rules of eye contact* described in the tip section (or the rules appropriate to the group you are with). You should consider creating a practice goal of establishing eye contact during meetings and conversations. A good exercise is to ask friends and family members to converse with you, face-to-face, and give you feedback about the duration and intensity of your eye contact. Another way to work on eye contact is to practice talking to yourself in the mirror while making eye contact with your own reflection. You can practice in this less challenging situation before working on eye contact with other people. If you change the way you typically make eye contact, you are likely to find it uncomfortable at first. With practice you will become more comfortable, and a normal level of eye contact will come to feel quite natural.

Another nonverbal behavior that enhances communication is nodding or saying "uh-huh" when someone is speaking. This shows you are listening carefully and understanding what he or she saying. (You actually do need to be listening to make this work! Saying "uh-huh" throughout a conversation while you are reading the morning paper will not win you any points.)

The Power of a Smile

Socially anxious people tend to smile infrequently. It seems harder to smile when you are feeling tense, and easier to smile when you let go of some of your tension. If you do not smile much in social interactions, you may want to practice smiling when you say hello to people. It is neither necessary nor desirable to grin like a used-car dealer on amphetamines. A brief smile—two or three seconds at most—usually works well. You might begin by smiling when you greet the people whom you see most often. Smiling is something you should list as a practice goal if it is something you need to improve.

Be a Good Listener

While it is certainly desirable to approach and speak to people at social occasions, you shouldn't feel pressured to say a whole lot—soliloquies work only in drama class. On the other hand, don't forget the value of being a good listener. When people are feeling troubled by a problem or excited by a personal triumph, they appreciate someone who listens to their story. The listener does not have to be able to solve the problem or speak knowledgeably about the triumph at hand; just listening seems to help in many situations.

An effective listener stays focused on what the other person is saying, makes eye contact and gestures such as head nods, and occasionally makes supportive comments or asks questions to help the person clearly describe his or her experiences, feelings, and opinions. Increasing your listening skills will help others appreciate you more.

Approaching Other People and Initiating Interactions

If you rarely initiate social interactions or conversations, this may be part of a pattern of avoidance. An alternative is to practice initiating brief interactions in as many social situations as possible. Saying good morning to the security officer in your building, waving at a neighbor when you're walking your dog, or greeting a fellow worker in the elevator can get the ball rolling. Even very brief comments delivered with a smile, such as "Hi, there!" "How are you today?" "Can you believe it's only Wednesday?" (this works best if it really is Wednesday), or "Have a good weekend!" (likewise, best used on Friday) can increase your social contacts and, ultimately, your social confidence. Avoid "I didn't know you were pregnant!" (she may not be) and "What a cute monkey!" (in case it's her older child).

Conversely, you may notice that someone is taking the trouble to say a few words to you. Your inclination may be to keep these interactions as short as possible—answering with just one or two words. If you are working to increase your comfort level in social interactions, don't rush through them. Take your time, say hello, and respond. This usually requires persisting in the interaction longer than feels comfortable to you in the beginning—time passes slowly when you're anxious. As you practice, you'll find that what seemed like an eternity of small talk was really just a minute or two, well within the realm of socially acceptable chitchat.

The Secret of Successful Small Talk: Learning to Say Dumb Things (Like the Rest of Us)

In our work with shy people, we have encountered two views about small talk that often get in the way of developing effective conversation skills. One view goes like this: "I really hate the small talk that you hear at a lot of social gatherings. It is so unimportant and it wastes so much time. I would rather talk to people about things that are important to me or not talk at all." The other view is: "I can't converse with people I don't know well. I just can't think of anything worthwhile to say."

TIP: REMEMBER NAMES.

People usually respond more warmly when you use their names. But you may not remember someone's name, or think you know but are afraid of making a mistake.

Remembering names takes attention and practice. You may not register someone's name when you are introduced, particularly if you're anxious. The remedy is to make sure you really pay attention when a person is being introduced and to repeat the name to yourself silently several times. If you didn't hear the name clearly, ask or repeat the name out loud: "I'm sorry, I didn't get your name; was that Genghis Khan or Candy Cane? Oh, nice to meet you, Candy!"

In a small business meeting, you may wish to write down people's names when introductions are made. During a quiet moment look at the faces and silently rehearse the names.

It's okay to be unsure about someone's name, and to admit to it: "Sorry, I know we've met but I've forgotten your name." Most people will appreciate the effort you make to identify them—especially since they may have forgotten your name, too.

When we hear people trying to avoid small talk this way, we let them in on the truth: small talk is like grease on the wheels of social interaction. Even though the topics involved may not be terribly important, small talk allows you to get conversations going. Small talk enables you to get to know people before you tackle more important business. If you do not go through the stage of making small talk, you will never get to the point of talking about things that are more important. Thus, the ability to make small talk is an essential part of being effective with people.

The Art of Conversation

Yes, conversation is an art. And like many artistic endeavors, some of us are going to be better at it than others. But there are things you can do to become more proficient at the art of conversation. You may not end up as a silver-tongued talk-show host, but you will improve your comfort level and effectiveness with people in general.

A challenge of conversation is finding something to talk about with a person whom you do not know very well. The classic approach of talking about the weather works well if there is a storm or heat wave, but at other times it can run out of momentum quickly. You can probably remember some of those conversations:

"We've sure been having weather lately."

"Yes, it never seems to end."

It is a good idea to have some other conversation starters for those days when the sun is shining and there's not a cyclone in sight.

There is a great acronym for conversation starters. (We didn't invent the acronym, nor do we remember who did, but we expect to hear from that person's lawyer any day now.) The word is *FORM*. It stands for *family, organizations, recreation,* and *money.* If you ask a question in any one of these areas, there is a good chance you will get the conversation rolling. If you know a few things about the person that will enable you to choose from among these topics, so much the better, but it's not necessary.

It's a good idea to spend a few minutes thinking of some conversation starters before you leave for a meeting or party. You can even write down a few on a card. Here are some examples:

♦ *Family*

Good Examples

How's the family?

Do you have any kids in school?

How are your kids doing?

How does your wife like her new job?

Bad Example

So, is this wife number three or four?

♦ *Organizations*

Good Examples

I was thinking of joining a gym. Do you know of any good ones?

What kind of projects are you working on these days?

This hotel has a terrific restaurant. Have you tried it?

Bad Example

Anything to do with politics or religion, unless you know the person's beliefs beforehand and don't plan on challenging them.

- ◆ *Recreation*

  Good Examples

    Are you going to (did you) have a chance to get away for a vacation this year?

    Did you have a good weekend? What did you do?

    Have you seen any new movies? What did you think of them?

    Did you notice the story in the paper about the honest lawyer? What did you think of it?

    Do you have any projects going on in your spare time?

  Bad Example

    My dog died. How about yours?

- ◆ *Money*

  Good Examples

    Can you believe how much gas prices have gone up?

    I'm thinking of buying a DVD player. Do you know much about them?

    I just finished doing my taxes. Does it seem to get more complicated every year, or is it me?

    Did you hear about that new service charge? What do you think about it?

  Bad Example

    Can you lend me fifty bucks?

TIP: EMPHASIZE THE POSITIVE.

Dale Carnegie, writing back in the 1930s, emphasized the importance of expressing a positive interest in people. Even if you don't have a strong interest in a person's favorite activity (nude beekeeping, for example), talking about the challenges of nude beekeeping can establish a relationship so you can talk later about interests you do have in common (hives, for example). An initial getting-to-know-you conversation is not the place to give negative opinions about another person's interests or beliefs.

It is often easier if you try to start the conversation with something you are somewhat familiar with, but this is not essential. Once you hit on a topic of interest, the conversation often takes off. Use follow-up questions to find out more about the people you are talking with and their interests.

You can learn a lot by listening to good conversationalists. How do they introduce themselves? What questions do they ask? Do they focus on themselves or the person they are speaking to? What patterns do you see in their eye contact, smiling, and other nonverbal behaviors? How does the conversation flow? How do they end conversations effectively? It is perfectly acceptable for you to imitate approaches that work well for other people. Over time, you can adapt them to your own conversational style.

TIP: KEEP A FILE ON PEOPLE YOU MEET.

You may find it useful to keep a file on people you meet. (We learned this tip from the CIA.) After a meeting or reception, commit the information to memory or, if you prefer, keep a paper or electronic file. Many electronic organizers have space to record additional information in their telephone and address files. When you meet new people, pay close attention to what they say about themselves. Try to remember some details about the person's family (spouse's name; how many children and their names and ages) and interests, and record the information later. This can be very helpful in future conversations, as it shows that you have taken an interest in whomever you have met. And this isn't just window dressing; it can be the basis for a real relationship. For example, you may have no interest in playing golf, but you might be able to derive great pleasure from hearing about someone's frustration with his last round!

Telephone Terror

At first blush, a telephone conversation seems less complicated and challenging than a face-to-face meeting. The telephone does have some unique challenges, though. When you contact people by telephone, you do not see their reactions as you do in a face-to-face situation. When you receive a call, your contact with the caller can come with little or no warning and leave you no time to prepare. Also, there is seldom enough time to exchange a lot of information.

Larry: "Don't call me and I won't call you."

Larry was a successful art director with a New York ad agency. He had had a stuttering problem earlier in life, but received help. He came across as an effective communicator. No one in his firm would have suspected that he was terrified of using the telephone, especially receiving calls. To mask his fear, he instructed the receptionist to direct calls to his voice mail and never to put a call through to him directly, even if the caller said it was urgent. He checked his voice mail frequently and would respond by e-mail whenever possible. Eventually, he relied almost exclusively on e-mail, to the point where clients began to complain that they could never talk to him.

He was able to overcome this problem by practicing taking some calls directly without preparation. He was able to handle many callers' inquiries immediately and told the others that he would get back to them. He also practiced and became more comfortable with making telephone calls to people in authority and in situations where he did not know what reaction to expect.

The telephone is an effective and economical way to communicate with people directly. It allows you to have more personal contact with people than either written or electronic (e-mail) communication. Using our antianxiety strategies works as well for the telephone as it does for face-to-face situations. If you have a difficult call to make, you can plan what you want to say and even prepare a written script for your side of the call. (If you are using a script, be sure to allow a lot of pauses to give the other person time to respond.) As you become more comfortable with telephone calls, make sure that you do not restrict yourself to calls requiring a script.

If telephone calls in general are difficult for you, it may be a good idea to return to Chap. 6 and identify some practice goals for making and receiving calls. The telephone is ubiquitous, so it should be easy to plan opportunities to practice your telephone skills.

Coping with Conflict

If you typically avoid conflict, chances are you've skipped this section and aren't reading this. But we hope you're still with us, because conflict is unavoidable. Some form of conflict (either constructive or destructive) is often a necessary part of solving problems. Coping with conflict is another essential interpersonal skill. Entire books are written about coping with conflict, and we can only touch on the high points here. (For a more detailed description of strategies for dealing with conflict, see the materials on assertiveness listed in the resources section at the end of the book.)

Here are five keys to coping with conflict:

♦ *Don't deal with conflict by avoiding it.* Some conflicts can be avoided, but many cannot. Avoiding a conflict will usually make it worse. You're better off dealing with it before it escalates into an explosion.

♦ *Be a good observer.* When do conflicts come up? Who is involved? What is the sequence of behaviors—on your part and the other person's part—that leads to conflict? What typically happens during the conflict? Is there a pattern in the emotional level of the participants? Does one person reach a state of high arousal first, and does the other person follow? What happens after the conflict, and how long does it take for the situation to seem relaxed again? When you are a good observer, you can often see patterns that may help you deal with conflict when it recurs.

♦ *Think about what you could do differently to influence the chain of behaviors between you and the other person.* When we think about interpersonal problems, we typically fantasize about how the other person should change. In reality, we have much more influence over our own behavior. If you change your behavior, you will influence the other person's behavior and change the pattern in the conflict.

♦ *Stay calm (not angry or frightened).* When you deal with angry teenagers, responding to their loud, shrill voices with a quiet, calm one is often effective in the long run. (In the short run it will also drive teenagers to distraction, which can be a nice side benefit.) It is also very important not to take personally the angry words of someone who is not coping well with conflict. If you wonder what others really think of you, it is best to pay attention to what they say and do when they are not angry. As you observe and develop strategies to deal with conflict, you will also find that many conflicts cannot be resolved on the spot by a logical discussion of the issues. Discussing the issues may be important, but often is ineffective unless it is done after the conflict has blown over.

♦ *Do not respond to conflict with violence against people or property.* If you respond to conflict with violence, you should seek professional counseling immediately. If someone has responded to conflict by acting violently toward you, you should report this to the police. This is very important—don't wait until the violence escalates to where someone is seriously injured

TIP: SEE CONFLICT AND ANGER AS A THUNDERSTORM.

One way to help yourself deal with a situation involving conflict and anger is to think of it as a thunderstorm. The situation may be full of thunder and lightning now, but if you handle things patiently, they will likely calm down soon. Pressing to solve a problem in the midst of a thunderstorm often escalates the difficulty.

Managing Anger: Mike

Jose and Vanessa had three children. The 10-year-old, Mike, often had difficulty getting along with other children at school. He liked to tease them but would become very upset when they teased back. When Mike arrived home from school he'd say things like "That kid was teasing me. I'm going to punch him in the face." Jose and Vanessa would explain to Mike that it wasn't smart to solve problems by fighting. They encouraged him to ignore the teasing and make sure he did not tease others. These explanations often ended in a shouting match and a slammed door as Mike stomped off to his room.

Jose and Vanessa would feel upset about the interaction. After some discussion, they decided to try handling the situation differently. When Mike came home in an angry mood, they would not respond to his extreme statements. Instead, they would ask him to tell them about the problem and how the school day had gone. Mike would tell his story and they would express regret that it had been such a tough day for him (without taking sides for or against the other kid). They made a point of staying calm and not making suggestions for how he could handle things differently, as he was not receptive to this. Before long, they found that Mike was settling down more quickly and they were not getting drawn into conflicts with him as often. They found that he was much more willing to listen to their advice at times when he was not upset.

Handling Criticism

Dealing with criticism is a challenge for us all, but it can be especially difficult for people with social anxiety. As is the case with conflict, receiving some criticism is a normal part of life. Being able to handle criticism effectively can be a real asset in dealing with people and reaching your own goals. One strategy for handling criticism follows many of the steps we just outlined for handling conflict. Here are some of the main points:

♦ *Do not put too much energy into avoiding criticism.* It is more effective to face the situation and solve the problem.

♦ *Once again, be a good observer.* What patterns do you see in situations where you receive criticism? Are the same persons doing the criticizing? Is the criticism reasonable? Is it constructive? Can it help you develop better ways to do things? How do you usually react to criticism? How do the other people in the situation respond to your reaction?

♦ *Try not to react too strongly to criticism and try not to take it personally.* If the criticism is appropriate, don't waste time and energy defending yourself or making excuses or apologies. A good response is "I goofed on that one. Let's see if there is some way we can sort it out quickly."

Coping with Criticism: Sharon

Sharon was the eldest of four children. As her mother entered her eighties, Sharon found she was spending more and more of her time caring for her. Her two sisters lived in different cities, and her brother, who lived in the same city, didn't spend much time with their mother.

Sharon's mother had always been critical of the girls in the family. She frequently criticized Sharon for not visiting enough and making poor choices when she picked up items at the grocery store. At the same time that she was critical of Sharon, she would speak in glowing terms of her son. Sharon was upset by the criticism and frustrated that her brother received such different treatment. She had tried many times to resolve the situation by discussing it with her mother, but this never seemed to get anywhere.

After reviewing her observations carefully, Sharon realized that her mother had always been very critical of the children and no amount of talking ever changed this. After talking to her brother and sisters, she realized that they were also aware of their mother's critical nature and that they did not take her criticisms seriously. Sharon considered minimizing her contact with her mother, but she felt that she wanted to continue to provide some support. In her view, the best approach was to work hard not to take the criticism personally and to underreact rather than overreact to it. Rather than explain to her mother that she was trying her best, she would just listen to the criticism, not respond to it, and change the subject. Sharon found that accepting her mother the way she was and not trying to change her was her best option. Dealing with her mother continued to be stressful, but she felt personal satisfaction knowing that she was caring for her.

Giving and Receiving Compliments

Receiving compliments can be uncomfortable (although not receiving them is worse). You may worry that people won't think you're modest enough. Or you may not like being the focus of their attention. When complimented on your new sweater, you may say something like "Oh, it's really six years old and there are holes in the elbows." This actually will draw *more* attention to you, and usually in a more negative way. The correct response to a compliment on your clothing or appearance is "Thank you for saying that, it was nice of you to notice." Or just plain "Thank you."

The other side of the coin is giving compliments. You may find this a bit awkward, although giving compliments is usually easier than receiving them. Giving a sincere compliment to someone is a great way to create a positive atmosphere and enhance a relationship. In everyday life, people often do not get as many positive responses as they deserve for their efforts. A compliment is usually much appreciated. It is easy to take the people closest to us for granted, and it is a good idea to compliment them generously. A compliment can also be a great conversation starter with someone you do not know well.

Practicing Your People Skills

Now that you have read this chapter on people skills, do you have any goals for improving your own? Take a few minutes to review the chapter to see if there are some areas that you should focus on. If so, take some time to plan specific activities to help move toward these goals, using the people skills worksheet in Fig. 12.1. Examples would be practicing eye contact, making a point of smiling when you say hello to people, approaching people to initiate conversations every day, or making phone calls to find out about joining a Toastmasters group. Remember that effective interpersonal skills are a great asset and worth practicing regularly. You may want to add these activities to your list of weekly practice goals for overcoming social anxiety.

TIP: KEEP PRACTICING!

Practice is the key to increasing your comfort in social situations. Remember to plan activities each week on your weekly practice sheet (Chap. 9). As you become ready, add to your weekly practice assignments some—or all—of the activities from the list you make on the people skills worksheet.

People Skills—Goals and Activities

1. Goal:

_____

Activities:

_____

2. Goal:

_____

Activities:

_____

3. Goal:

_____

Activities:

_____

4. Goal:

_____

Activities:

_____

5. Goal:

_____

Activities:

_____

6. Goal:

_____

Activities:

_____

Figure 12.1   People skills worksheet.

CHAPTER 13

Broadening Your Circle of Friends

How Important Is It to Have Friends?

How many friends do you need? Researchers who study health, illness prevention, and the ability to cope with illness consistently find that people who have more friendships and more positive relationships with both friends and family are healthier—both physically and mentally. They are more satisfied with life in good times and cope more effectively when problems arise.

Taking Stock of Your Friendships

Think about the people you consider friends; don't include romantic relationships.

Now answer these questions:

1. How satisfied are you with the *number* of nonromantic friendships you have?

1	2	3	4
Very dissatisfied	Somewhat dissatisfied	Somewhat satisfied	Very satisfied

2. How satisfied are you with the *quality* of your nonromantic friendships?

1	2	3	4
Very dissatisfied	Somewhat dissatisfied	Somewhat satisfied	Very satisfied

3. Do you consider yourself difficult or easy to get to know?

1	2	3	4
Very difficult	Somewhat difficult	Somewhat easy	Very easy

4. How comfortable are you in getting close to people?

1	2	3	4
Very uncomfortable	Somewhat uncomfortable	Somewhat comfortable	Very comfortable

5. How difficult or easy is it for you to trust people?

1	2	3	4
Very difficult	Somewhat difficult	Somewhat easy	Very easy

Now add up your score. The total will range from 5 to 20. The higher the score, the better you perceive the quantity and quality of your friendships and your capacity for intimacy. If you scored 15 or higher, you're a paragon of friendship and trust! If you scored between 10 and 15, you're doing well with your friendships, but there is room for improvement. If your score is 10 or lower, you have work to do to improve the extent and quality of your friendships.

It can also be useful to take stock of how often you are in touch with friends and family. Ask yourself how often you participate in the activities listed in Fig. 13.1 (check the box that most closely represents your situation).

Would You Benefit from Having More Friends?

You are the best judge of whether you would like more friendships. As you consider this, remember that people with more social support generally have better physical and emotional health. Why is this? Social contacts often involve you in pleasurable activities that combat stress and are a source of satisfaction. Friends and family provide practical support for life's everyday demands. When you are facing serious life problems, they

How often do you participate?

Activity	Daily or almost daily	1–3 times a week	1–3 times a month	Less than once a month	Never
Get together with a friend or friends, either in your home or theirs.					
Get together with a friend or friends, neither in your home nor theirs.					
Keep in touch with a friend by phone or letter.					
Get together with a neighbor or neighbors for a chat.					
Get together with relatives.					
Keep in touch with relatives by phone or letter.					

Figure 13.1   Activity involvement checklist.

provide advice and emotional support, as well as help with daily chores like babysitting, cooking, and going to the market.

Typical friendships vary in different phases of life. Young people, whose main focus is on finding fulfilling careers and appropriate life partners, tend to socialize with other young people. Parents with young children interact with other families with young children. Parents with teenagers typically find that their children spend more time with friends and less time with family. In this phase of life, parents are wise to invest more energy in their own friendships so they do not become isolated and suffer from empty-nest syndrome as their children grow up. In each stage of life, you benefit from having a solid circle of friends.

If you think you would benefit from having more friends, read the rest of this chapter and plan activities to meet this goal. If not, skim these pages and move on to the next chapter.

Basic Assumptions About People

People have different assumptions about trust. Some believe that most people can't be trusted. They believe that if people have a chance they will criticize you, make negative comments about you, or reject you. Other people have a different view. They believe that most people can be trusted and that trust is a matter of degree. They believe that most people are kind and not terribly critical of their neighbors and colleagues. For these people, it is not hard to decide whether to have lunch or coffee with a coworker. What could be so risky about that?

But it takes longer to decide whether you can trust someone to take care of your home when you are away or care for your children for a day. This higher degree of trust is established through knowing a person over a period of time and seeing how he or she acts toward others.

Life is less stressful if you believe that most people can be trusted to a reasonable degree. If you are able to trust most people, you don't have to keep so many secrets. If people know about you—that you are shy, or that you wish you were more physically fit, or that you aren't wealthy—most can be trusted not to use this information in a harmful way. If someone responds negatively to you, perhaps you do not need that person as a friend.

If you have trouble trusting others, you may worry that people may *gossip* (share your secrets) with others. When we checked the definition of *gossip* in our *Funk and Wagnalls Dictionary,* here is what we found: "1. idle, often malicious talk, especially about others, 2. informal, chatty talk or writing as of personages, social events, etc." Just as people pass the time by watching other people, they also pass the time by discussing them. This is normal and not meant to hurt anyone. There are always a few people who talk about others in a hateful way. Others often recognize this negative slant and do not take it seriously. A person who talks about others in malicious ways is not the kind of person you want as a friend, nor the kind you care to impress.

On the other hand, we all have issues we prefer to keep private. Someone with good interpersonal skills will respect the privacy of others. If you speak positively about people and respect their privacy, your friendships will prosper.

Taking a Gamble, Learning to Trust

Sharing information about yourself is a key aspect of trust. You may worry that if others learn something about you they do not agree with or that you consider unflattering, they will think less of you. Part of developing a close friendship is sharing information about your life, even aspects that are not perfect. This happens gradually as friendships develop, and it is a two-way street.

Craig: "I'm embarrassed about my son's problem."

In working to overcome his shyness, Craig was spending more time with his colleagues at coffee breaks and lunch. People often spoke about their children. At these times, he felt uncomfortable because his son had learning problems and was an unmotivated student. He worried that his son would never finish high school. When he listened to others talking about their children's school and sports achievements, he wondered whether he and his wife were poor parents.

One day, Craig took a chance, discussed his worries with his colleagues, and was surprised when his supervisor mentioned that his daughter was also having problems at school. As time went on, he found that taking risks and sharing information allowed him to feel more comfortable and become closer to his friends.

Some personal situations are more difficult to talk about than others.

Greg: "Will people accept me?"

Greg was a 33-year-old accountant who had been socially anxious since high school. He avoided interactions with colleagues and, when he sat with them at coffee breaks, would listen but say very little about himself.

One source of Greg's discomfort was his homosexuality. He lived with his partner of eight years, and hiding this had always been stressful. He worked for a large bank with good protections against discrimination. Two women in his office were openly homosexual and had not experienced negative consequences.

In order to become more comfortable with his coworkers, Greg decided he would gradually let people know about his living situation. Most of his coworkers accepted his homosexuality; others were less comfortable. Greg decided that since he was comfortable with his sexuality, he didn't have to worry about whether everyone approved. After the initial stress of letting down his guard, Greg found he was much more comfortable. He developed stronger friendships at work because he was finally able to talk about his life.

People have very different opinions on issues such as sexuality, politics, religion, work, interests outside of work, and family life. You can be good friends with someone even if you disagree about who should be president or which team deserves to win the World Series.

Looking for the Perfect Friend?

Maria: "I have no friends."

Maria was a retired teacher with a wide range of social and volunteer activities. She played bridge on Tuesdays and Thursdays, and volunteered three times a week at a church soup kitchen. We were therefore surprised when she told us she had no friends. She felt she had many acquaintances, but no one she considered a friend. She had known these acquaintances for a long time and had joined them in a variety of activities, including two overseas trips with a woman in her bridge group. After our discussion, we came to two conclusions. First, her expectations of a friend were so high, it would be difficult for anyone to make the grade. Second, she would benefit from working on closeness and trust.

Friendships are established over time. When you first meet someone, it is hard to predict how a friendship might develop. Most of us can benefit from friendships with varying levels of intensity. Some friends you may see at coffee breaks, others may be neighbors you see occasionally for lunch, and still others may be people you go out with to a movie, a concert, or a game. As you talk more about your lives, you may become close friends. Similarly, close friendships may diminish in intensity over time as interests and life circumstances change.

Reconnecting with Friends from the Past

If you want to increase your friendships, one place to start is by reconnecting with friends with whom you have lost touch. Many of us can go for years without seeing a good friend, but feel the years melt away once we make contact. The same can apply to relationships with brothers, sisters, and other family members. You may have lost touch when the relationship was not going well, yet you may still be able to mend the relationship in the future. Be prepared for things not to work out well or for the other person to be uninterested. Also, the relationship may not be as close as it was before, but may still be worthwhile.

Marianne: "My friends dropped me."

Marianne, a 43-year-old science teacher, was unusually sensitive to rejection. The previous summer, she had been depressed, and consequently avoided her friends. As this year's summer break approached, we encouraged her to be more socially active.

One of the contacts she was considering was with Helen, a woman in her neighborhood who had been a good friend in the past. They enjoyed shopping, walking, and going for lunch. When we asked how the friendship dropped off, Marianne said she was not sure. She felt disappointed that she was the one who usually made the first contact. She stopped calling Helen and waited to see if Helen would call her; Marianne hadn't heard from her in some time. When Marianne was feeling anxious or low, she frequently turned down invitations, and Helen may have stopped phoning for this reason.

Marianne thought at first that Helen would not want to hear from her. When we asked why she felt this way, Marianne acknowledged she had no evidence and could only know this if she could read minds. We agreed that she would contact Helen with an invitation for lunch. Marianne and Helen spent two hours at lunch catching up, and they were able to pick up where they had left off.

Marianne's story also raises the issue of who initiates contact—in other words, who tends to call first. People may cut off friendships because the other person does not initiate. In friendships, it is preferable that people take turns calling first. In the real world, however, some people are more organized and effective at initiating interactions. It is helpful to develop your skills in this area. You may have good friends who are not good at initiating, but the friendship is so rewarding, you don't mind calling most of the time.

Friendships may be imbalanced in other ways. One person may always pay for lunch, host the get-togethers, or plan the activity. Rather than end the relationship because of this, you can suggest handling things in a more balanced way—splitting the check, eating at restaurants rather than going to someone's house, or alternating who chooses which film to see.

Establishing New Friendships

People find new friends everywhere: chatting at work, walking their dogs, mingling with the other parents at their children's preschool. People also make friends through clubs, adult education programs, religious groups, volunteer programs, and sports. Make a point of talking to people you meet in these situations. Ask them about their interests, their jobs, their families—and tell them about yours. These casual conversations are the stuff of which successful friendships are made.

You should also know the patterns people follow in developing relationships. In the workplace or at school, friendships often start casually at coffee breaks, lunches, and meetings. The next step is to arrange to get together after work for a drink, a baseball game, a movie, or a community lecture. Next, arrange to meet at your home or your friend's home for a cup of coffee or a meal.

TIP: BECOME AWARE OF THE DIFFERENCES IN MEN'S AND WOMEN'S FRIENDSHIP PATTERNS.

Men and women differ in the ways they spend time with their friends. Generally, men structure friendships around activities—sports, outdoor experiences, work, and hobbies. Women generally structure their friendships around getting together and talking—either in person or on the telephone. If you're aware of these differences, you can better plan your social practice assignments.

Cliques

Some people feel discouraged about developing friendships at work or school because of *cliques*. What is a clique, anyway? The *Funk and Wagnalls Dictionary* has a clear explanation: "Clique, coterie, and circle denote a group of persons having a common interest. Clique suggests that this interest is selfish or hostile to a larger group, whereas coterie suggests amiable congeniality. A circle centers on a person or an activity, and may be small or large: a sewing circle [for example]." So, viewing people who get together regularly as a *clique* has negative connotations and suggests they are selfish, perhaps because they want to keep others out of the group. What looks from the outside like a clique may look from the inside like a group of friends who enjoy spending time together. Don't assume that you won't be welcome if you ask to join them. Try it. Take the risk. If you're rebuffed, you can move on to join other groups, or establish your own.

Friendship Goals

Now that you've read this chapter, do you think you would benefit from having more friends? If so, plan specific activities to achieve this goal, using the friendships worksheet in Fig. 13.2. Contact a former friend and arrange to meet for coffee, or invite a colleague to a barbecue at your house, or join your coworkers for lunch. Add friendship activities to your weekly practice assignments.

TIP: FRIENDSHIPS TAKE TIME TO DEVELOP.

Friendships deepen as you share your thoughts and feelings with others, and they grow to trust you and share theirs with you. This takes time. Plan practice assignments each week to strike up new friendships and deepen the ones you already have.

TRAP: Don't be paralyzed by fear of rejection.

When you reach out to people and invite them to join you for activities, it's natural for some of them to decline. Don't take it personally. Keep working to develop a variety of friendships and expect some disappointments along the way. After all, if you invite a coworker to join you for lunch and get a *no, thanks,* it doesn't mean she doesn't like you. She may have other plans; she may be short of money and prefer to bring lunch; or she may be attending AA meetings at noon. Who knows—she may even have social anxiety!

Friendships—Goals and Activities

1. Goal:

   _____

   Activities:

   _____

2. Goal:

   _____

   Activities:

   _____

3. Goal:

   _____

   Activities:

   _____

4. Goal:

   _____

   Activities:

   _____

5. Goal:

   _____

   Activities:

   _____

6. Goal:

   _____

   Activities:

   _____

Figure 13.2   Friendships worksheet.

CHAPTER 14

Spicing Up Your Social Life

Developing a more active social life can help you spark new friendships and improve the ones you have. Even if you have enough friends, you may find that you do not have as much social contact or excitement as you would like to have. (Our idea of fun was writing this book, so it doesn't take much to excite us. You may have higher expectations.)

Stop Saying No to Invitations

You may have become accustomed to quickly saying no, thanks to invitations. You do not have to accept every invitation, but you should consider each one and whether the activity would help you overcome your social anxiety. Get in the habit of saying yes to invitations that immediately interest you, and "May I think about it and get back to you?" to the rest. After considering the pros and cons, say yes to as many as possible that would help you face your fears.

Horrors: Inviting People to Your Home

A cornerstone of social life is visiting someone's home. This can be an economical way to socialize, especially if you have young children. (If your kids are like ours, they will provide the entertainment, whether you would like them to or not, and you don't have to pay a babysitter, at least if you're the host).

You may be horrified by the prospect of inviting someone into your home. You may imagine that visitors will be secretly critical of your house-keeping ("What a pig!"), your taste in furnishings ("What a pig!"), and your cooking ("What, no pig?"). You visualize many hours of cleaning house and preparing food before you could allow visitors into your home. You worry about how people will respond to unruly children or pets (or spouses). This can be even more challenging when you have visited friends who have opulent homes and serve gourmet meals.

How can you deal with the challenge of having others visit your home? A first step is to be aware of your negative thoughts about having visitors. Write these down, question how realistic they are, and develop coping thoughts. Remember that when you invite people over, their agenda is not usually to perform a home inspection. Reduce the pressure by opting out of any sense of competition about the food or drinks you serve, the housekeeping and house furnishings, and even the activities. Not every-one is a gourmet cook or an interior designer, and not everyone needs to be.

Make the visit comfortable by keeping things simple and making sure that you (the host) have time to socialize. Here are some ways to do this:

♦ Plan small gatherings, especially if you have not been comfortable having guests to your home.

♦ Make the gatherings as informal as possible.

♦ Keep the cleaning up before the visit to a reasonable level. If your guests seem preoccupied with miniscule amounts of dirt in your home, recommend that they read a good self-help book on obsessive-compulsive disorder.

♦ Prepare a basic meal—something you would serve your own family, not something you can't even pronounce (although we must admit that we do enjoy a good *pomme de terre avec du beurre* now and again). Prepare in advance so you can socialize when people are visit-ing. Pick up ready-made or ready-to-make dishes from the grocery or bakery rather than trying to prepare everything yourself. Consider potluck, where each visitor brings one dish.

♦ Whenever possible, arrange for people to serve themselves food and drink. Some socially anxious hosts use meal preparation and serving as a way to avoid social contact—are you one of them?

- A barbecue or outdoor meal is especially good because it is easy to keep the menu and preparation simple. An alternative is to arrange a picnic; the local flora and fauna can make an excellent topic of conversation when the weather is boring ("Sally, is that an African fire ant on your knee?")

- If you know the people well, have them help you prepare the meal— good friends enjoy socializing while they help slice tomatoes for a salad, or open a bottle of wine.

- Consider planning an activity such as watching a rental movie together or going for a walk in the neighborhood.

- Leave the cleanup until after your guests have gone. (Although preparing the meal together can be fun, even the best of friends will balk at cleaning up.)

Most of us learn our entertaining style from our parents or, worse, from the movies. Develop your own style of having visitors, preferably one that is low key and, therefore, low stress. The more you invite people to your home, the more they will reciprocate. This means more times when you can go to someone else's house and watch them sweat.

Having a Plan for Every Weekend

Your social calendar may be thin because you do not plan activities ahead of time. You think about activities for Saturday night on Saturday afternoon, and at that point it may be too late to arrange to meet with friends. You may always get together with the same friends without reaching out to new ones. If this is a problem for you, plan two or three weeks ahead for an activity every weekend. Vary the activities and the people. Your local newspaper, magazine, Web page, or community center may have a guide to local entertainment. Many community activities, such as book signings and library concerts, are free or low in cost.

Using Personal Interests to Develop Social Contacts

Developing your personal interests can help increase your social contacts and friendships. Think of activities where you can work toward two goals at once—increasing your fitness (or knowledge, or hobby skills) while increasing your social contacts. Choose activities where you are likely to meet the kinds of people who interest you. Be ready to say yes or "May I think about it and get back to you?" when you're invited somewhere. Also be prepared to invite people to join you in an activity. Here are some examples:

- Adult sports activities such as baseball, soccer, hockey, bowling, cycling, hiking, or walking. Or, if you're particularly masochistic, golf. Find an activity or team that suits your level of skill and competitiveness. Do the activity for the fun of it, rather than for the opportunity to be perfect at it.

- Fitness activities, such as classes at YM/YWCAs or local clubs and gyms. You are more likely to strike up a conversation with people who are attending a regular class than you are with those who are using facilities on their own.

- Hobby classes and clubs (music, chess, bridge, photography, foreign language, dance) arranged by community centers and educational organizations.

- Cooking classes. Preparing food can be the center of an enjoyable get-together.

- Continuing education programs ("Learn to make others anxious: Become an IRS auditor").

- Volunteer activities arranged by community, political, or religious groups.

- Nature and outdoor activities.

- Travel activities arranged by community organizations.

When you participate in an activity, you automatically have something in common with the other people attending. Often they will get together for coffee or a snack before or after the activity. Remember to join in when this happens, and even initiate a gathering yourself.

Contact with Neighbors

It is not unusual to see neighbors for years without saying anything to them other than the occasional "Shut your dog up" and other such pleasantries. Investing time and energy in getting to know some of your neighbors can be a tremendous source of social contact and potential friendships. Usually this starts with just stopping to say a few words ("Nice dog. Loud, but nice."), then longer conversations ("Your dog has quite a vocabulary. I don't think I've ever heard a dog with quite so much to say. You must be proud of the little beast."), then an invitation for coffee ("Why don't you drop by for coffee sometime when your dog is tied up?"), and then perhaps an invitation for a meal ("I'll feed your family for the next year if you send your dog to a farm in another state").

You might arrange to have a few neighbors over for an informal gathering to get to know them better. You are likely to have some things in common with your neighbors. Don't let differences in age or family situation prevent you from making contacts. People of different ages often have a lot to offer each other. Neighborhoods are more comfortable and even safer when neighbors know one another and talk regularly.

Contact with Family Members

Families are often spread all over the continent. If some family members live where you can have regular contact, they can be a part of your social activities. You start off with some things in common, which may make it easier to develop a relationship. You may also have to change some of the ways you have related in the past. Young people who were often invited to a parent's home can invite their parents over or plan some activities away from home. Siblings who have lived through childhood rivalries may have to try out new activities and leave rivalries behind. You may have to spend time getting to know more distant relatives just as you would new friends. If your family lives far from you, you may have to keep in touch by telephone or e-mail between visits.

TIP: INVEST IN RISKY BUSINESS.

You take a risk every time you ask someone to join you for lunch, go bowling, or sign up with you for a stock-picking course. The risk is that she'll say no, or things won't go splendidly and he won't reciprocate in the future. Is this a risk worth taking? You be the judge. But consider the alternative— doing things alone.

Goals and Activities to Stimulate Your Social Life

Have you set any goals oriented toward spicing up your social life? If so, plan specific activities to move toward these goals, using the social life worksheet in Fig. 14.1. Some examples would be inviting a neighbor for a snack, joining a fitness class, inviting friends over for an informal dinner, or phoning a family member to arrange a get-together during the kids' summer vacation. Great relationships don't come from a single meeting, so plan regular activities to allow time for friendships to develop.

TRAP: **Remember: not everyone has to like you.**

You may be disappointed when you initiate a social activity and don't hit it off with the other person or persons involved. You may blame yourself for not fitting in. Remember that not everyone has to like you. Last time we counted, there were several billion people in the world. If you can find something in common with just a few of them and you nurture the relationships, your social life will be rich indeed.

Social Life—Goals and Activities

1. Goal:

   _____

   Activities:

   _____

2. Goal:

   _____

   Activities:

   _____

3. Goal:

   _____

   Activities:

   _____

4. Goal:

   _____

   Activities:

   _____

5. Goal:

   _____

   Activities:

   _____

6. Goal:

   _____

   Activities:

   _____

Figure 14.1 Social life worksheet.

CHAPTER 15

Letting Love Find a Way: Romance

Romantic Relationships: Good News and Bad News

A survey by our colleague Carrie Lionberg found that under half the people coming for help with social anxiety were in romantic relationships, as compared to over two-thirds of another group without anxiety problems. The good news is that most people surveyed—both socially anxious and not—were happy with their romantic relationships.

Are You in a Relationship Already?

A healthy romance requires continuous effort. You may develop a pattern where one partner encourages contact with friends and family, while the other tries to cope with anxiety by avoiding contact. This pattern may cause conflict and limit the fun you and your partner have. Enjoying activities together is one of the best ways to maintain and improve your relationship. Including friends and family in your leisure activities (from going to a movie to taking a vacation) helps produce more variety and interest.

Barry: "Different strokes for different folks."

My wife and I have enjoyed traveling ever since we first met. While we enjoy doing things together, we also have many different interests. When we visit another city, she enjoys window-shopping and browsing the stores. When I have been shopping for a short while, I quickly feel exhausted. On the other hand, I can spend many hours visiting museums—but after a short time in a museum, my wife starts to have back pain.

We have solved these problems by splitting up for part of the day and each doing his or her favorite thing. This works even better when we travel with or visit friends. It is easy to divide into groups and enjoy different activities. We get together for meals and evening events. We enjoy each other's company even more when we are sharing our experiences with friends and have breaks from each other.

Some people feel that their life partner should be their closest friend, and that they should have all of their needs fulfilled by that one person. People who rely on a romantic relationship to meet all their needs for social support may put great strain on the relationship. People who have a broader range of friendships tend to have better romantic relationships, too.

Learning to Walk Before You Run

People often feel rushed to become romantically involved before they are comfortable with a person as a friend. There is a real advantage to taking things one step at a time. Friendship requires many of the same capacities as romance—learning to trust, extending invitations, expecting some declined invitations, planning social activities, and giving the relationship time to develop. Working on friendships is an excellent way to prepare for romantic relationships. Participating in social activities with friends is an excellent way to meet dating partners.

Romantic relationships are more challenging than friendships for many reasons:

- ♦ *More people are available for friendship than romance.* Finding the right person to date is more formidable than finding someone to have lunch with. You are likely to date many people before you find the right person for a continuing and deepening intimacy.

- *Often you have to make several invitations to arrange a date.* Declined dating invitations can be more discouraging than those declined by nonromantic acquaintances. Coping with disappointment and rejection requires well-developed interpersonal skills and self-confidence.

- *Romantic relationships are more complicated than friendships.* There is more possibility of misunderstanding and hurt feelings if problems arise. Expect challenges to come up, and do not take all problems personally.

- *It takes time for a romantic relationship to develop.* A relationship that looks positive initially may not work in the long run. Bringing a romantic relationship to an end, or turning it into a friendship, can be awkward and painful.

Developing a Romance

Much has been said about what it takes to establish a good romantic relationship. It is a challenge to give advice in the short space we have available. On the other hand, our wives might tell you that we could put everything we know about successful dating approaches on half a page. Fortunately, in our work we have many opportunities to learn about other people's experiences.

Much of what we said about friendship also applies to romance. You are most likely to meet potential dating partners in your neighborhood, at school, at work, and through regular social and leisure activities. You are also more likely to meet dating partners if you participate in a variety of activities than if you are waiting at home for the telephone to ring. Choosing activities where you are likely to meet potential dating partners is the first step. Focus on activities you will enjoy even if you do not meet someone. If you feel happy about your life, your friends, and your activities, you are more likely to meet a dating partner. If you are waiting for someone to come along and rescue you from an unhappy life, you are less likely to meet someone suitable. In fact, you risk meeting someone who is downright unsuitable.

Here are some general observations about dating:

- *Men are still more likely than women to ask for the first date.* In a study of college students, 78 percent of men indicated they had made the first contact that led to a romantic relationship, while 45 percent of women indicated that they had initiated a relationship. That being said, it is completely appropriate for a woman to ask for a date.

- *People tend to like and date people who have interests and opinions similar to their own.* In general, opposites do *not* attract.

- *Physical attractiveness seems to be important to both women and men.*

- *People tend to like others who express a liking for them.* Emphasizing the positive in your interactions typically creates a friendlier atmosphere. Likewise, most people are sensitive to criticism and will not respond warmly if you express disapproval of their ideas or values. We're not suggesting that you be dishonest with people, merely that you emphasize positive rather than negative feelings until you've reached a deeper level of trust.

- *Relationships grow stronger as people find activities they enjoy together.*

- *College students often report that their first successful interactions involved just talking, in person or on the telephone.* These interactions involve disclosing personal information, opinions, and beliefs.

- *Many people report that friends or family were involved in arranging a first meeting.* Few people report having a successful romance whose early encounters involved the use of alcohol or drugs. This questions the strategy of trying to meet people at a bar. (Bars attract people with drinking problems, as well as personal problems.)

- *Most college students say they experience moderate to high levels of anxiety when they ask someone out on a date.* Anxiety is a normal part of dating.

Tracey: "I want to start dating."

Tracey was a painfully shy 31-year-old physiotherapist. Her main weekend activity was helping her mother, a widow, on the family farm two hours from her apartment. Since she was out of town almost every weekend, she missed many social activities with her colleagues. Tracey came to us because she wanted to start dating; she felt she was missing out on life.

Tracey agreed with us that it would help if she could spend more weekends in the city. She was concerned that her mother would be too lonely if she did not visit every weekend, but after they discussed it, her mother encouraged her to spend every second weekend in the city and to keep in touch by telephone.

Tracey felt very nervous around men, especially those she was attracted to. There was one young man she was drawn to, but she had never been able to ask him out. Tracey feared she might never find someone to share her life.

The challenge of dating is so overwhelming that some people just can't get started. A helpful way to cope is to break down the challenge into smaller steps, as outlined in Chap. 9. Here are some steps we suggested for Tracey:

♦ *Conversation is especially important during dates.* Practice talking to people similar to the kinds of people you would like to date. Practice with many different people—even if they are not available for dating. You may find it easier to start with someone who is not available, as this reduces the pressure to successfully ask her or him out.

♦ *Place more emphasis on joining social activities at work and among friends and family.* Be sure to participate actively—initiate conversations, ask questions, suggest an activity for the following week. Friends and family may be the ones who introduce you to a potential dating partner.

♦ *Consider joining a structured activity such as a club or team, or sign up for a course.* Participate in activities where you would be likely to meet people who are interested in the same things you are.

♦ *Participate in a variety of leisure activities.* Attend movies, concerts, sports, and special events, so you can suggest an enjoyable activity when you date.

♦ *It is important for both men and women to be able to initiate a date.* If you are a woman, you don't need to wait for a man to ask first.

♦ *When you make invitations, expect some to be declined.* People who are successful in the long run learn to be persistent and to not take declined invitations personally.

♦ *Expect to date a number of different people before you discover the right one.* It is rare to find a life partner after only a few tries.

If dating is challenging for you, expand your horizons by picking up a book on dating techniques. Some good ones are: *Be Your Own Dating Service* and *Date Lines: Communication from "Hello" to "I Do" and Every-*

thing in Between, both by Nina Atwood. The full references are in the resources section.

TIP: TAKE CHANCES WITH YOUR AFFECTION.

Just as starting a friendship involves developing trust, starting to date involves risking your affection. You may worry that you will invest your emotion and it may not turn into a long-term romantic relationship. It is helpful to be philosophical here. One quotation seems to fit particularly well. Tennyson wrote in the poem *In Memoriam A.H.H.* in 1849, describing the death of a close friend:

>'Tis better to have loved and lost
>Than never to have loved at all.

TRAP: Don't leave your friendships behind.
You may become so involved in a romance that you neglect your friendships. Remember that friendships are important for a balanced life. Allow time for both you and your romantic partner to maintain friendships.

Looking for the Perfect Partner

Some people are reluctant to date someone they do not consider a potential lifelong partner.

Jason: "I can't meet anyone who appeals to me."

Jason was a very shy customs officer in his late twenties. In the past he had been a regular at a local bar, hoping to meet someone, but had to stop when he developed a drinking problem. Then, a young woman he met through a friend asked him for a date. Jason and Donna went out to the movies and enjoyed the evening, but Jason wasn't sure if he should call her for another date. Donna didn't have a model's figure and wasn't the kind of person he would have considered asking out. In fact, he had experienced problems in the past when he had been interested in a strikingly attractive woman and then felt too intimidated to ask her out.

We suggested to Jason that, rather than look for the perfect woman, he should consider dating various women before settling into a relationship. Taking a more relaxed approach would allow him to become comfortable with the activities involved—phoning a woman, planning an activity, and especially making conversation (something he found especially difficult). Jason decided to take this approach and found that as he spent more time with Donna, he enjoyed her company more and more. He dated one other woman but came back to Donna. As time went on, Jason and Donna's relationship developed into a satisfying romance.

Most people do not settle down with the first person they date, finding that a more relaxed approach helps them become comfortable enough to date many people, until they meet someone special.

TIP: DON'T WAIT UNTIL YOU'RE PERFECT TO START DATING.

Just as some people are looking for the perfect partner, others do not want to start dating until they have achieved perfection themselves. You may want to lose weight, firm up, get better clothes, have a nicer car, and so on, before you start to date. While it is important to take care of your appearance if you want to meet people, it is even more important to accept and like yourself the way you are. You can start dating while you continue to improve yourself.

Telephone and Internet Relationships

With technology developing rapidly, more people are developing friendships through telephone dating services and Internet chat rooms. While it's great to have more ways to meet people, you should be aware of the advantages and disadvantages of these methods. An advantage is that you can meet many more people. Indirect meetings may be less anxiety arousing, and you can get to know each other to some degree before the challenge of a face-to-face meeting. A disadvantage is that you only get to know certain aspects of the person with whom you are corresponding. It is normal and desirable to be on your best behavior when you meet someone new. As time goes on and you see people in a variety of situations, you learn more about their strengths, weaknesses, and personal characteristics, and they learn the same things about you. When you communicate only on the Internet or by telephone, the content is more controlled, and you do not have the opportunity to learn as much about the other person.

In real life it is important to pay attention to a person's actions, not just his or her words, and you are deprived of this opportunity when you use the Internet or telephone as your main method of contact. A solution may be to use the telephone or Internet early in a relationship, and then progress to face-to-face meetings. When you do arrange that first meeting, use good judgment and meet in a public place, preferably with a group of people you already know.

TRAP: **Don't overuse the Internet.**

Some people get so caught up in making contacts through the Internet that they neglect making contacts close to home. We know people with friends in Russia, Ireland, and Australia who have few or no friends in their own cities. While making friends who live in other regions is an exciting experience, it is also important to meet people you can visit without buying a plane ticket. There are many activities you can enjoy with local friends that you cannot share with your Internet friends. Have you ever tried bowling on the Web?

Being a Happy Single Person

Many relationships break up, and many marriages end in divorce. Don't make your happiness depend on being in a romantic relationship. Many single people are very happy with their lives. If you are unattached, put energy into having a satisfying and enjoyable life as a single person. This approach pays off if you remain single or if an opportunity for a relationship comes your way.

Goals for Your Romantic Life

What goals do you have concerning romantic relationships? Take a few minutes to review this chapter and identify areas you might focus on. Plan specific activities to move toward these goals, using the relationships worksheet in Fig. 15.1. Remember that great relationships don't come from a single activity or one-time meeting, so plan regular meetings to allow time and opportunity for relationships to develop.

TIP: PLAN REGULAR PRACTICE.

Practice is the key to progress. Be sure to plan activities each week on a copy of the weekly practice sheet (Chap. 9). When you are ready, include activities from the relationships worksheet in your practice assignments.

Relationships—Goals and Activities

1. Goal:

   _____

   Activities:

   _____

2. Goal:

   _____

   Activities:

   _____

3. Goal:

   _____

   Activities:

   _____

4. Goal:

   _____

   Activities:

   _____

5. Goal:

   _____

   Activities:

   _____

6. Goal:

   _____

   Activities:

   _____

Figure 15.1   Relationships worksheet.

The Topography of Progress: Peaks, Plateaus, and Valleys

Y ou probably lived with social anxiety for some time before taking steps to overcome it. It's great that you made the decision to face it head-on. You've been following the recommendations in this book, and have made progress toward your goals. Now you can sit back and relax, right? Guess again!

Even after you've made headway toward overcoming your social anxiety, an even bigger challenge can be to maintain and improve upon your initial gains. In this epilogue we will review some of the challenges that are likely to arise as you work toward a lasting triumph over shyness.

Plateaus

It is common when you learn a new skill to make a lot of progress early on and then level off at a *plateau.* There are several reasons why this so often occurs. You may feel comfortable with the improvement and not go on to more formidable goals. Or you may become busy with other activities and not focus on social anxiety. In any case, it is common to reach a plateau and still have considerable work to do to overcome the problem.

Speaking Up but Not Joining In: Lisa

Lisa was age 33, married, and the mother of two elementary-school-age children. Lisa had spent most of her adult life paralyzed by social anxiety. She worked as a homemaker—cooking, shopping, and chauffeuring her children to and from school and other activities. What little free time she had was spent alone, as she was terrified of talking to others. Over the years, her unwillingness to interact with other mothers had earned her a reputation as a snob, something Lisa did nothing to refute as it provided her with a good cover for her social avoidance.

One day Lisa's younger daughter asked, "Mom, why are you afraid of the other moms?" Lisa was devastated, but rather than sulk, decided to do something about her problem. She bought a self-help book written by two brilliant therapists (no relation), and dedicated herself to following their program for three months.

Within weeks, Lisa was talking to other mothers in the parking lot, making play dates for her children, and volunteering to answer phones in the school office. She was delighted with her progress.

But after four months, Lisa noticed that her progress had leveled off. Although she was able to speak with others more comfortably than she had ever imagined possible, she realized that she still was unable to get close to them. Though she had spoken to dozens of other parents, she had not established a single friendship. Lisa wondered if she still appeared aloof, and whether that might be pushing other people away. She pulled out her self-help book and decided to reread the sections on relationships. She also promised herself that if she didn't make headway in the next two months, she would find a therapist to help her over this bump in the road.

Areas of avoidance and excessive anxiety that remain unchallenged can be seeds of future problems. Often we are not motivated to move on from a plateau to a higher level of functioning until a new challenge comes up— a promotion, a new relationship, or a problem in an old relationship. It is important, as soon as you can, to put renewed energy into moving toward overcoming your remaining problems with social anxiety. Don't wait for a special occasion—or a crisis—to arise.

Setbacks

Life and anxiety have something in common: progress is never completely smooth in either. You may, for example, feel less anxious talking to the gas-station attendant one week and more anxious the next. These ups and downs are normal.

It is also normal to experience *setbacks*. A setback is when, after a period of progress, your anxiety or avoidance increases again. During a setback, you typically also feel less confident about your ability to cope. This can be quite discouraging, especially if you didn't think it could happen. Setbacks happen to everyone at one time or another. Now you know!

Sometimes it's impossible to figure out why you're experiencing a setback. If that's the case, your job is to crack open this book, rededicate yourself to your goals, and formulate a plan to keep moving toward them. At other times, though, you may be able to identify specific factors that contribute to a setback. Being aware of these factors should help you to cope and come up with a strategy for overcoming the setback. Here are some common examples of situations that can contribute to setbacks:

♦ Any experience that gives you a feeling of failure, such as making a major mistake in an assignment at work or school, falling seriously behind in your work, getting into an argument with a colleague or friend, or being criticized by a supervisor or family member

♦ Disruption in a relationship, such as a close friend moving away or breaking up with a boyfriend or girlfriend

♦ A new responsibility in your life that you do not feel prepared to handle, such as a promotion at work, or a new baby on the way (even happy developments can cause setbacks)

♦ Extra stress in your life from personal illness or an illness in the family, financial pressure, or an unusually heavy workload

From Knocking on Doors to Knocked Down (but Not Out): Josh

Josh was a 42-year-old pharmaceuticals salesman. He had the sometimes difficult job of calling on doctors to promote and provide information about medications manufactured by his company. Most of the time Josh enjoyed the stimulation of talking with bright people about their work. But he sometimes found it stressful trying to arrange appointments with the doctors, which required that he be assertive with their receptionists to get past the standard "Dr. Lecter is too busy to meet with you" response.

Josh had experienced social anxiety for many years. He had a long-standing fear of public speaking, which he believed restricted his advancement at work. He was uncomfortable at parties and at times had coped by drinking excessively. He frequently awoke with hangovers and had missed so many days of work that he worried about getting fired. About a year and half earlier, he had worked with a counselor who focused on his drinking and introduced him to a social phobia self-help book.

After two months of restricting his alcohol intake and practicing the relaxation and conversation techniques in the book, Josh could comfortably attend business functions without drinking. He was happy with his progress but still had not dealt with his fear of public speaking. He considered joining Toastmasters but just didn't seem to have the time.

Things were going well when a friend asked Josh to be best man at his wedding. Josh knew this would involve proposing a toast, something he dreaded. He became preoccupied with the upcoming wedding and, in the ensuing weeks, started feeling anxious again at parties. When he found himself craving a drink, Josh feared he was in trouble.

Josh's situation is a clear example of a setback. His friend's invitation to be best man was a vote of confidence in him (good news), but the situation required him to take on challenges he had been avoiding. Josh had wanted to become comfortable with public speaking for many reasons but now was forced to take it on before he felt ready. At first he didn't realize why he was feeling more anxious than usual, but when he stopped to think about it the situation was clear. Just understanding why this was happening made it easier to cope.

Josh decided to call his therapist, who reminded him that setbacks were the rule rather than the exception. He suggested that Josh use the wedding as an opportunity to refresh some of the coping strategies he had learned earlier. Josh reread the chapter on controlling physical symptoms of anxiety and recalled that the relaxed breathing approach had helped him before. He brushed up on the technique by closing his office door and listening to his relaxation tape twice a day. He also reviewed the material on using effective coping thoughts and

> **TRAP:** **Don't make a setback into a catastrophe.**
>
> Some people feel like giving up when they experience a setback. They say things like "I'm right back at square one" when in fact they have made a lot of progress. Even when you feel you have lost a lot of ground, you can usually regain it quickly because of your previous learning. When working on overcoming anxiety, it is best to keep setbacks in perspective—even seemingly significant ones. They are seldom as serious as they seem.

realized that he had been catastrophizing about the toast. He countered these thoughts by reminding himself, "People aren't there to judge me. They're there to see my friends get married. They'll smile and applaud anything I say!"

Josh decided it was best to cope with the wedding toast by breaking it into smaller steps. He joined Toastmasters, even though he knew he would not have time to complete the program before the wedding. Just going to the meetings made him anxious, and this was a good way to get used to facing his fear. He prepared his speech well in advance and practiced in front of a couple of trusted friends.

The day of the wedding came. Although Josh was very anxious before the toast, it went off without a hitch, and several people came up afterward to congratulate him. He was proud of how he had handled his setback, and particularly pleased that it had motivated him to work on becoming a more confident and comfortable public speaker.

This approach of stopping to understand the reasons for a setback and then developing a plan to deal with it can be applied to many situations.

TIP: USE YOUR PAST SUCCESSES.

You may suffer a setback and feel you have to look for an entirely new solution to a problem. This is usually unnecessary. Instead, consider strategies (for example, developing effective coping thoughts) that have been helpful in the past. You are usually most familiar with these and can readily put them into practice. It may be best to consider new approaches once you have overcome the setback.

Troubleshooting

> ▶ *You have tried to overcome your anxiety in a situation but are still finding it difficult.*

When people make limited progress, the problem is usually that they have not practiced enough in difficult situations. Some challenging situations (such as confronting an annoying coworker or asking your boss for a raise) do not come up frequently. At times, people expect to see significant improvement after just a few practice sessions, when in fact it may take a lot of practice over an extended time for their skills to improve. Think of our earlier example of learning to swim. It takes many hours of practice to become a better swimmer. Similarly, increasing your confidence in social situations may take many practice sessions. In both cases, the practice pays off with the development of a long-lasting skill.

When you are facing a situation that does not come up frequently, such as speaking in front of a large crowd, it may be helpful to break it into steps, and then practice each step repeatedly (see Chap. 8). When Josh planned for the toast, he practiced the steps before the wedding. He could also, had he thought of it, have hosted a small party prior to the wedding in order to practice his speaking skills in front of a smaller audience. It can take some creativity, but almost any situation, however rare, can be broken down into elements that can be practiced repeatedly.

> ▶ *You have been facing a situation repeatedly, but you still feel very anxious.*

In spite of repeatedly going into a challenging situation, some people notice little decrease in their anxiety level. A detailed review of the situation often identifies one of two problems. The first is that subtle forms of avoidance can prevent you from fully participating and developing a sense of confidence and mastery. To review, here are some common examples:

♦ You go to school or work every day but avoid talking to people around you.

♦ You avoid eye contact with the teacher or the person leading the meeting so that you will not be asked a question.

♦ At work or school you avoid invitations to go to coffee or lunch, or you go only with one or two familiar people.

- You listen to people in a discussion but <u>avoid giving your opinion</u> because you are afraid of saying something foolish or stumbling over your words.

- You will go to a social gathering only if someone you know well is there with you. You may rely on that person to do most of the talking.

- You meet one or two people at a social gathering, spend the whole time with them, and <u>avoid speaking to others</u>.

- You worry about spilling your beverage, so you <u>avoid drinking</u> in front of others, or you drink only those beverages in containers with lids and straws.

In each of these cases, your actions—sometimes called *safety behaviors*—prevent you from being fully involved in the situation. Although you use these strategies to help you cope, they prevent you from having as wide a range of options for your actions as you would otherwise have. <u>The solution is to work</u> toward letting go of these safety behaviors and participating fully in the situation.

A second problem occurs when, even though you are practicing a situation frequently, <u>you maintain your anxiety by thinking negatively</u> (see Chap. 7). Common problem areas include building up your anticipatory anxiety by predicting that a situation will go badly, being overly focused on yourself rather than on others, and evaluating your performance negatively during and after a situation. One way to see if negative thinking is a problem for you is to complete a thought diary after a difficult situation. If negative thinking is a problem for you, review the approaches outlined in Chap. 7.

▶ *You have a disappointing experience with someone close to you.*

As we've said before, establishing new relationships and renewing old ones involves taking risks and learning to trust. When you open yourself to others, it is normal to be disappointed sometimes. Here are some examples:

- Your brother agrees to see a movie with you but changes his mind at the last minute. You feel disappointed and hurt.

- Your supervisor disagrees with you about a hiring decision. You give in, fearing confrontation.

- During a moment of anger, your friend says things that hurt you. It is hard to let go of your hurt feelings and not take the comments very personally.

- Someone you have been dating doesn't want to continue seeing you. You are devastated.

Some people respond to disappointment or rejection by quickly cutting off relationships, deciding it is not safe to trust people, or by feeling hopeless about the possibility for better outcomes in the future. It is important to be able to continue to work on relationships even when you encounter disappointments. If possible, try not to take these disappointments too personally, but rather expect them as part of the normal give and take of life. Few people are perfect, and it is easier to get along if you are able to accept other people's imperfections. It is also best not to end relationships hastily, even when you encounter a disappointment. For more help, review the keys for coping with conflict (Chap. 12).

Goals for Maintaining Your Progress

Now that you have finished this section, do you have goals for maintaining and furthering your progress? Take a few minutes to review the material to see if there are some areas you could focus on. Then take 5 or 10 minutes to formulate your goals, and another 10 to 15 minutes to plan specific activities to move you toward them, using the maintenance worksheet in Fig. E.1.

Remember the importance of persistence and regular practice. If you decide to expand your circle of friends, for example, think about different ways to do it. Is there a class you can take where you might meet people? Are there people you already know whom you could get to know and trust more—could you, for example, ask a colleague to join you in your favorite weekend sport? Is it time to call an old friend you haven't seen in years? Whatever the goal, make sure the activities you propose are both specific and repeatable.

Maintenance—Goals and Activities

1. Goal:

_____

Activities:

_____

2. Goal:

_____

Activities:

_____

3. Goal:

_____

Activities:

_____

4. Goal:

_____

Activities:

_____

5. Goal:

_____

Activities:

_____

6. Goal:

_____

Activities:

_____

Figure E.1. Maintenance worksheet

The Topography of Progress: Peaks, Plateaus, and Valleys   203

Afterword

Writing this book has been an adventure for both of us. It has forced us to take what we have been doing for years in our practices and our research and distill it into these few pages. In so doing, we have had the wonderful opportunity to reassess what we do, why we do it, and whether it is the best way to do it. This has been at times challenging, frightening, and enlightening (rarely all at the same time). Never has it been boring. We've had a great time writing this book. We hope that reading it proves to be even a fraction as enjoyable for you.

We believe that the advice contained in this book will help you triumph over social anxiety in the short term and stay well in the long term. We hope that we're right. Please let us know.

Before we conclude, we want to reiterate the key steps to overcoming social anxiety:

1. *Decide to do something about it.* The path of least resistance is to let anxiety rule your existence. Don't make concessions to it. Take control, fight back, and unlock your life.

2. *Choose the treatment that's right for you.* There is more than one road to success. If medication suits your style, find an experienced physician and start treatment. If you prefer to work with a therapist to tackle your anxious thoughts and avoidance, then choose a ther-

apist and begin. If you want to work on the problem on your own, follow our self-help program and stick to it.

3. *Be flexible.* Not all treatments work well for everyone. If you're not making progress, be prepared to change gears and investigate a different approach.

4. *Be patient.* Change takes time. You didn't suddenly wake up socially anxious one morning. Anxiety won't vanish overnight. Praise yourself when you progress toward your goal. Don't beat yourself up when things move slowly.

5. *Practice makes perfect.* "Perfect" is probably a poor choice of words. Perfection is not the goal; progress is. If you have the courage to put yourself in situations that make you anxious, and you have the tenacity to stay there long enough for your discomfort to subside, you *will* get better.

6. *Let others into your life.* Yes, some people are jerks. But you've got to accept the premise that there are good people out there, people worth knowing, people worth trusting. Take the necessary risks and find those people, and let them find you.

Now get out there and do it!

Resources

Audio and Video

Freedom From Anxiety. *Jerilyn Ross (2001). Chicago: Nightingale-Conant. Available through www.RossCenter.com.*

At-home, self-help version of a program offered at the Ross Center for Anxiety and Related Disorders in Washington, D.C. Particularly useful for social phobia, specific phobia, and panic disorder. Includes audiocassettes, videocassette, workbook, and resource guide.

Books

Anger

The Anger Workbook. *Lorrainne Bilodeau (1992). Minneapolis, MN: CompCare.*

A very practical and insightful approach to anger management. Explains how to understand and transform anger by working through a series of exercises and questionnaires.

The Dance of Anger: A Woman's Guide to Changing the Patterns of Intimate Relationships. *Harriet G. Lerner (1997). New York: Harper Trade.*

Bestseller that explores how women can improve their relationships by learning to recognize and appropriately express anger. Deals with specific anger situations, such as those involving partners, parents, children, and families.

Anxiety

The Anxiety and Phobia Workbook (3d ed.). *Edmund J. Bourne (2000). Oakland, CA: New Harbinger.*

Provides information and exercises to master coping skills. Has a strongly holistic approach, and includes sections on the body, self-esteem, and spirituality.

Feel the Fear and Do It Anyway. *Susan Jeffers (1992). New York: Fawcett.*

A 10-step program designed to help you channel fear, indecision, and anger into empowerment. Has excellent sections on visualization and imagery, power vocabulary, and optimism.

Triumph Over Fear: A Book of Help and Hope for People with Anxiety, Panic Attacks, and Phobias. *Jerilyn Ross, with preface by Rosalynn Carter (1995). New York: Bantam Doubleday Dell.*

A practical and inspirational guide to understanding and overcoming anxiety problems.

Assertiveness and Communication

The Assertive Woman (3d ed.). *Stanlee Phelps & Nancy Austin (1997). San Luis Obispo, CA: Impact.*

Offers help with body image, attitude, power, compliments, saying no, and anger. Explores possible scenarios and response strategies.

Your Perfect Right: A Guide to Assertive Living (7th ed.). *Robert E. Alberti & Michael L. Emmons (1995). San Luis Obispo, CA: Impact.*

A bestseller emphasizing the development of better communication skills for assertiveness. Contains questionnaires, step-by-step learning procedures, and information on related topics such as anger, school, the workplace, and the family.

Body Dysmorphic Disorder

The Broken Mirror: Understanding and Treating Body Dysmorphic Disorder. *Katharine A. Phillips (1998). New York: Oxford University Press.*

Describes and suggests treatment options for body dysmorphic disorder (BDD), a condition in which people are preoccupied by what they feel is a defect in their appearance.

Children's Anxiety

Helping Your Anxious Child: A Step-By-Step Guide for Parents. *Ronald M. Rapee, Susan H. Spence, Vanessa Cobham, & Ann Wignall (2000). Oakland, CA: New Harbinger.*

As it promises, provides step-by-step approach. Illustrations can be understood by children. Many useful and practical examples. Uses plain language. One of the best books for parents.

Keys to Parenting Your Anxious Child. *Katharina Manassis (1996). New York: Barron's Educational Series.*

This book is briefer than the one by Rapee and colleagues. Less detail about techniques. Has a good section on medication and coaching for parents when dealing with professionals.

Dating and Romantic Relationships

Be Your Own Dating Service: A Step-By-Step Guide to Finding and Maintaining Healthy Relationships. *Nina Atwood (1996). New York: Henry Holt.*

Atwood, a therapist, provides details on how to handle the dating process from first steps to the development of a healthy romantic relationship, with emphasis on creating a full, rewarding life as a single person. The book provides step-by-step information about how to search for the right partner.

Date Lines: Communications from "Hello" to "I Do" and Everything in Between. *Nina Atwood (1998). New York: Henry Holt.*

A follow-up to the author's previous book (preceding listing), this one puts more emphasis on communication in dating and developing a healthy romance. Very practical and down-to-earth advice. The very specific information and coaching (including ideas for wording when dealing with difficult topics) should be helpful for people with social anxiety.

Depression

Feeling Good: The New Mood Therapy. *David D. Burns, with preface by Aaron T. Beck (1999). New York: William Morrow.*

Self-help book on overcoming depression. Emphasizes cognitive-behavioral techniques. Depression is frequently a problem for people with anxiety disorders.

Mind Over Mood: A Cognitive Therapy Treatment Manual for Clients. *Dennis Greenberger & Christine A. Padesky (1995). New York: Guilford Press.*
  Designed to be used independently or in the context of cognitive therapy for depression.

Friendships

How to Start a Conversation and Make Friends. *Don Gabor (2001). New York: Simon & Schuster.*
  Practical advice about initiating contacts and developing friendships.

General Mental Health

Authoritative Guide to Self-Help Resources in Mental Health. *John C. Norcross, John W. Santrock, and others (2000). New York: Guilford Press.*
  Comprehensive description of self-help resources including books, videos, and Web sites. Designed for professionals, but may be helpful to general readers as well.

Caring for the Mind: The Comprehensive Guide to Mental Health. *Dianne R. Hales, Robert E. Hales, & Allen Frances (1996). New York: Bantam.*
  Easy-to-read, comprehensive guide to mental health, treatments, and medications. Lists how a particular disorder feels, how it appears to others, when to seek help, risks and complications, and long-term outcomes. Special chapters on children, the elderly, and families.

Panic Disorder

Don't Panic: Taking Control of Anxiety Attacks. *R. Reid Wilson (1996). New York: HarperCollins.*
  A widely used book by an author with a strong interest in self-help approaches.

Master Your Panic and Take Back Your Life!: Twelve Treatment Sessions to Overcome High Anxiety (2d ed.). *Denise F. Beckfield (1998). San Luis Obispo, CA: Impact.*
  Self-help book based on principles of cognitive-behavioral therapy.

Parenting

How to Talk So Kids Will Listen and Listen So Kids Will Talk (20th ed.). *Adele Faber & Elaine Mazlish (1999). New York: Avon.*

An easy-to-read and very successful instructional guide to parent-child communication.

1-2-3 Magic: Effective Discipline for Children 2 to 12 (2d ed.). *Thomas W. Phelan (1996). Minneapolis, MN: Child Management.*

In a very entertaining manner, Phelan shows why parent-child communication must be different from adult-adult exchanges. Provides excellent suggestions for promoting and discouraging various behaviors.

Paruresis (Shy Bladder Syndrome)

Shy Bladder Syndrome: Your Step-by-Step Guide to Overcoming Paruresis. *Steven Soifer, George D. Zgourides, Joseph Himle & Nancy L. Pickering (2001). Oakland, CA: New Harbinger.*

A remarkable book offering a practical and well-designed program.

Shyness and Social Phobia*

Diagonally Parked in a Parallel Universe: Working Through Social Anxiety. *Signe A. Dayhoff (2000). Placitas, NM: Effectiveness-Plus Publications.*

Covers everything from soup to nuts. Written from an insider's perspective, with humor and empathy.

Dying of Embarrassment: Help for Social Anxiety and Phobia. *Barbara G. Markway, Cheryl N. Carmin, C. Alec Pollard, & Teresa Flynn (1992). Oakland, CA: New Harbinger.*

Our all-time favorite until our own book came along! Provides a good description of the kinds of problems faced by socially anxious people, along with solid advice about how to get help and move forward.

The Hidden Face of Shyness: Understanding and Overcoming Social Anxiety. *Franklin Schneier & Lawrence Welkowitz (1996). New York: Avon.*

A well-researched and well-written book on the topic. Provides many interesting case vignettes and loads of good information and advice.

Painfully Shy: How to Overcome Social Anxiety and Reclaim Your Life. *Barbara G. Markway & Gregory P. Markway (2001). New York: St. Martin's.*

*Yes, there *are* other books on the subject . . .

A marvelous resource for people working to overcome problems with social anxiety. Comprehensive, thoughtful, and exceedingly well written.

The Shyness and Social Anxiety Workbook: Proven Techniques for Overcoming Your Fears. *Martin M. Antony & Richard P. Swinson (2000). Oakland, CA: New Harbinger.*

A highly readable self-help book with practical recommendations to help overcome shyness and social anxiety.

Substance Abuse

The Recovery Book. *Al J. Mooney, Arlene Eisenberg, & Howard Eisenberg (1992). New York: Workman.*

Detailed prescription for recovering from addiction; also of interest to family members and friends. Discusses how to choose treatment, possible obstacles to recovery, and relapse prevention.

Internet

The authors suggest the following Web sites as potential sources of information and support, but cannot be liable for the content or quality of information provided by the sites.

American Psychiatric Association
1400 K Street NW
Washington, DC 20005
Phone: (202) 682-6220, (888) 357-7924
Web site: www.psych.org

Professional organization representing many psychiatrists in the United States. Site describes symptoms of anxiety disorders, their causes, and related conditions. Links to other sites are listed, and resource materials can also be ordered from the site.

American Psychological Association
750 First Street NE
Washington, DC 20002-4242
Phone: (202) 336-5500
Web site: www.APA.org

Professional organization representing many psychologists in the United States. Displays online information brochures and gives some general tips for coping with some of life's day-to-day problems. Also provides a phone number to call to be referred to a psychologist in your area.

Anxiety Disorders Association of America (ADAA)
11900 Parklawn Drive, Suite 600
Rockville, MD 20852-2624
Phone: (301) 231-9350
Web site: www.adaa.org
E-mail: anxdis@adaa.org

Organization devoted to helping people with anxiety disorders. Site describes the different types of anxiety disorders and provides detailed information about both medication and various forms of psychological treatment. Also offers a self-test for social anxiety and databases listing professional therapists and self-help networks according to location.

Association for Advancement of Behavior Therapy (AABT)
305 Seventh Avenue, 16th Floor
New York, New York 10001-6008
Phone: (212) 647-1890
Web site: www.aabt.org

Professional organization dedicated to behavior therapy research and treatment. Site includes a geographical listing of professional therapists, their contact information, and which disorders they treat. The head office also provides pamphlets about specific disorders and guidelines for getting treatment.

Canadian Psychological Association (CPA)
151 Slater Street, Suite 205
Ottawa, Ontario K1P 5H3
Canada
Phone: (888) 472-0657
Web site: www.cpa.ca

Professional organization representing many psychologists in Canada. Provides information about several disorders, including anxiety disorders. Provides general descriptions, key features, causes, and treatments. Also provides a list of psychologists according to location.

Duke University Program in Child and Adolescent Anxiety Disorders (PCAAD)
Director: John S. March, MD, MPH
Department of Psychiatry, Box 3527
Duke University Medical Center
Durham, NC 27710
Phone: (919) 684-4950
Web site: www2.mc.duke.edu/depts/psychiatry/pcaad/

University-based clinic and research program for anxious youth. Site discusses anxiety disorders in children and adolescents.

Freedom From Fear
308 Seaview Avenue
Staten Island, NY 10305
Phone: (718) 351-1717
Web site: www.freedomfromfear.org

Organization dedicated to helping persons with anxiety problems. Site provides a self-test questionnaire that can be reviewed by a professional therapist and discussed with the respondent either over the phone or in person. Also provides a database of related associations, organized by zip code.

International Paruresis Association
P.O. Box 26225
Baltimore, MD 21210
Phone: (800) 247-3864
Web site: www.paruresis.com

Organization devoted to furthering the understanding and treatment of paruresis. Offers useful information on shy bladder syndrome and what can be done to help.

National Institute of Mental Health, National Institutes of Health
5600 Fishers Lane, Room 15C05
Rockville, MD 20857
Phone: (301) 443-4513
Web site: www.nimh.nih.gov/anxiety

U.S. government agency that funds and promotes mental health research and treatment. Site provides basic facts about anxiety disorders and describes key features of each. Gives general information about available treatments. Also provides addresses and links to Web sites of other mental health organizations.

Selective Mutism Group Childhood Anxiety Network (SMG-CAN)
Director: Elisa Shipon-Blum, DO
1130 Herkness Drive
Meadowbrook, PA 19046
Phone: (215) 887-5748
Web site: www.selectivemutism.org
E-mail: DrESBaskthedoc@aol.com

Nonprofit organization dedicated to selective mutism and related childhood anxiety disorders.

The Shyness Institute
Directors: Lynne Henderson, PhD, and Phil Zimbardo, PhD
2000 Williams Street
Palo Alto, CA 94306
Phone: (650) 493-6398
Web site: www.shyness.com

Private treatment center specializing in shyness. Site describes shyness and social phobia at length and provides a list of organizations offering treatment and information. Persons interested in participating in research projects may complete online questionnaires.

University of California San Diego (UCSD) Anxiety and Traumatic Stress Disorders Program
Director: Murray B. Stein, MD
Department of Psychiatry (0985)
University of California San Diego
La Jolla, CA 92093
Phone: (858) 622-6124
Web site: www.veryshy.com

University-based clinical research program situated in the Department of Psychiatry, University of California, San Diego. Includes information about shyness and social anxiety—descriptions, treatments, resources, and links.

Medication Information

Web MD
Web site: www.webmd.com

Consumer information section has section on medications with details on prescription drugs.

Public Speaking

International Training in Communication (ITC)
2519 Woodland Drive
Anaheim, CA 92801
Phone: (714) 995-3660
Web site: www.itcintl.org

ITC provides public-speaking training. Web site describes organization's basic goals and geographical and historical information. Provides links to Web sites of chapters in different countries.

Toastmasters International
P.O. Box 9052
Mission Viejo, CA 92690
Phone: (949) 858-8255
Web site: www.toastmasters.org

Organization devoted to helping people improve their public-speaking skills. Site describes the services Toastmasters offers. Services can be tailored to meet specific needs. Site also provides a database of existing Toastmasters groups worldwide. Also offers public speaking tips.

References and Sources

In writing this book we have distilled and synthesized information from many sources. Much of the content is the fruit of many hours of conversation with students, friends, and colleagues at home and abroad. And all of the content has been influenced by the professional presentations and writings of the many experts who study and treat shyness and social anxiety.

The titles that follow are those published works that are referenced in the text or include factual information alluded to therein. We have also included seminal textbooks that contain much of the information we cited. Many other works have undoubtedly influenced us, and we apologize if we have neglected to cite those influences here.

American Psychiatric Association (1994). *Diagnostic and Statistical Manual of Mental Disorders* (4th ed.) (*DSM-IV*). Washington, DC: American Psychiatric Press.

Beidel, D. C., & Turner, S. M. (1997). *Shy Children, Phobic Adults: Nature and Treatment of Social Phobia.* Washington, DC: American Psychological Association.

Dugatkin, L. A. (2001). *The Imitation Factor: Evolution Beyond the Gene.* New York: The Free Press.

Heimberg, R. G., & Becker, R. E. (in press). *The Nature and Treatment of Social Fears and Phobias.* New York: Guilford Press.

Heimberg, R. G., Liebowitz, M. R., Hope, D. A., & Schneier, F. R. (Eds.). (1995). *Social Phobia: Diagnosis, Assessment, and Treatment.* New York: Guilford Press.

Heimberg, R. G., Liebowitz, M. R., Hope, D. A., Schneier, F. R., Holt, C. S., Welkowitz, L. A., Juster, H. R., Campeas, R., Bruch, M. A., Cloitre, M., Fallon, B., & Klein, D. F. (1998). Cognitive behavioral group therapy vs. phenelzine therapy for social phobia. *Archives of General Psychiatry, 55,* 1133–1141.

Hofmann, S. G., & DiBartolo, P. M. (2000). *From Social Anxiety to Social Phobia: Multiple Perspectives.* Needham Heights, MA: Allyn & Bacon.

Kessler, R. C., Stein, M. B., & Berglund, P. (1998). Social phobia subtypes in the National Comorbidity Survey. *American Journal of Psychiatry, 155,* 613–619.

Leary, M. R., & Kowalski, R. M. (1995). *Social Anxiety.* New York: Guilford Press.

Liebowitz, M. R., Gorman, J. M., Fyer, A. J., & Klein, D. F. (1985). Social phobia: Review of a neglected anxiety disorder. *Archives of General Psychiatry, 42,* 729–736.

Magee, W. J., Eaton, W. W., Wittchen, H. U., McGonagle, K. A., & Kessler, R. C. (1996). Agoraphobia, simple phobia, and social phobia in the National Comorbidity Survey. *Archives of General Psychiatry, 53,* 159–168.

Mendlowicz, M. V., & Stein, M. B. (2000). Quality of life in individuals with anxiety disorders. *American Journal of Psychiatry, 157,* 669–682.

Miller, R. S. (1997). *Embarrassment: Poise and Peril in Everyday Life.* New York: Guilford Press.

Physicians' Desk Reference (55th ed.) (2001). Montvale, NJ: Medical Economics.

Rosenbaum, J. F., Biederman, J., Bolduc-Murphy, E. A., Faraone, S. V., Chaloff, J., Hirshfeld, D. R., & Kagan, J. (1993). Behavioral inhibition in childhood: A risk factor for anxiety disorders. *Harvard Review of Psychiatry, 1,* 2–16.

Rubin, K. H. (Ed.). (1993). *Social Withdrawal, Inhibition, and Shyness in Childhood.* Hillsdale, NJ: L. Erlbaum Associates.

Sapolsky, R. M. (1998). *Why Zebras Don't Get Ulcers: An Updated Guide to Stress, Stress-Related Diseases, and Coping.* New York: W. H. Freeman.

Schmidt, L. A., & Schulkin, J. (Eds.). (1999). *Extreme Fear, Shyness, and Social Phobia: Origins, Biological Mechanisms, and Clinical Outcomes.* New York: Oxford University Press.

Schneier, F. R., Liebowitz, M. R., Abi-Dargham, A., Zea-Ponce, Y., Lin, S.-H., & Laruelle, M. (2000). Low dopamine D_2 receptor binding potential in social phobia. *American Journal of Psychiatry, 157,* 457–459.

Stein, M. B. (Ed.). (1995). *Social Phobia: Clinical and Research Perspectives.* Washington, DC: American Psychiatric Press.

Stein, M. B., Fuetsch, M., Muller, N., Höfler, M., Lieb, R., & Wittchen, H.-U. (2001). Social anxiety disorder and the risk of depression: A prospective community study of adolescents and young adults. *Archives of General Psychiatry, 58,* 251–256.

Stein, M. B., Fyer, A. J., Davidson, J. R. T., Pollack, M. H., & Wiita, B. (1999). Fluvoxamine in social phobia (social anxiety disorder): A double-blind, placebo-controlled clinical study. *American Journal of Psychiatry, 156,* 756–760.

Stein, M. B., & Kean, Y. (2000). Disability and quality of life in social phobia. *American Journal of Psychiatry, 157,* 1606–1613.

Stein, M. B., Liebowitz, M. R., Lydiard, R. B., Pitts, C. D., Bushnell, W., & Gergel, I. (1998). Paroxetine treatment of generalized social phobia (social anxiety disorder): A randomized controlled trial. *Journal of the American Medical Association, 280,* 708–713.

Stein, M. B., Torgrud, L. J., & Walker, J. R. (2000). Social phobia symptoms, subtypes, and severity: Findings from a community survey. *Archives of General Psychiatry, 57,* 1046–1052.

Stein, M. B., Walker, J. R., & Forde, D. R. (1996). Public-speaking fears in a community sample: Prevalence, impact on functioning, and diagnostic classification. *Archives of General Psychiatry, 53,* 169–174.

Tangney, J. P., & Fischer, K. W. (Eds.). (1995). *The Psychology of Shame, Guilt, Embarrassment, and Pride.* New York: Guilford Press.

Van Ameringen, M., Lane, R. M., Walker, J. R., Bowen, R. C., Chokka, P. R., Goldner, E., Johnston, D. C., Lavalle, Y. J., Nandy, S., Pecknold, J. C., Hadrava, V., & Swinson, R. P. (2001). Sertraline treatment of generalized social phobia: A 20-week, double-blind, placebo-controlled study. *American Journal of Psychiatry, 158,* 275–281.

Zimbardo, P. G. (1990). *Shyness: What It Is, What to Do About It.* Cambridge, MA: Perseus Books Group.

Index

About the Authors

Murray B. Stein, MD, FRCPC, is a professor of psychiatry at the University of California San Diego (UCSD), and director of the Anxiety and Traumatic Stress Program at UCSD and at the Veterans Affairs San Diego Healthcare System. His research interests include social phobia, panic disorder, and posttraumatic stress disorder. He has published over 150 articles on these topics in professional journals such as *The Lancet* and the *Journal of the American Medical Association.* He is also a member of the Scientific Advisory Board of the Anxiety Disorders Association of America. He lives in San Diego.

John R. Walker, PhD, is a registered clinical psychologist and director of the Anxiety Disorders Program at St. Boniface General Hospital in Winnipeg, Canada. He is also a professor of clinical health psychology at the University of Manitoba and supervises senior clinical psychology students in their training in treatment of anxiety disorders. He is an editor of *Panic Disorder and Agoraphobia: A Comprehensive Guide for the Practitioner* and has written chapters on social anxiety disorder and treatment of intense illness worries. He has a special interest in self-help approaches to the treatment of anxiety disorders and has completed treatment evaluation studies demonstrating the benefits of self-help materials in treating panic disorder and social phobia. He lives in Winnipeg.